HARDEN'S

London for Free

Other Harden's titles
London Restaurants 2004
UK Restaurants 2004
Hotel Guide 2004
Good Cheap Eats in London 2004
London Bars & Pubs
London Food Shops
London Baby Book

For further information on any of the above, please call
(020) 7839 4763 or visit www.hardens.com.

© Harden's Limited, 2003

ISBN 1-873721-49-8

British Library Cataloguing-in-Publication data:
a catalogue record for this book is available from
the British Library.

Printed and bound in Italy by
Legoprint

Research Manager: Antonia Russell
Prodution Manager: Elizabeth Warman
Additional research by Sarah Ashpole & Nicola Semple

Harden's Limited
14 Buckingham Street
London WC2N 6DF

Contents

Introduction

What can you do in London for free?

World-famous parks, beautiful ancient woodlands, great museums and galleries, spectacular annual events and superb entertainments – the capital has an unrivalled range of free attractions.

As you will see, whatever your age and interests, whether you're a parent with children to entertain, a Londoner wanting to explore or a visitor to this great city, you really can do a lot of wonderful things here without paying a penny.

Is everything in this book really absolutely free?

Yes. Except where clearly stated to the contrary, everything in this book is free of charge. The only qualification is that if an asterisk (*) appears next to a name this means that free access is restricted in some way. The attraction may be free only at certain times (in which case the times we give in the small print are only those when there is no charge), or, in a few cases, you may not have access to the whole building. Many of the capital's larger free-access museums and galleries hold occasional special exhibitions for which there is a charge.

Just in case there is any confusion, where shops, markets, pubs or cafés are mentioned, they are included because they offer great window-shopping opportunities or because we thought it would be helpful for you to know about them. Sadly, there's a charge for the goods and services they offer.

Transport (Shanks's pony aside) also must be paid for. We would recommend any visitor to buy a Transport for London Travelcard – they are very good value and once you have one you can zip around the capital with no regard to expense. Daily Travelcards can be bought af 9.30am and, subject to zone restrictions, allow unlim transport on buses, tubes, Docklands Light Railway Tramlink trains.

Organisation

How is the book laid out?

First, geographically. We've split London into six areas, starting with Central (which is mainly the area usually called the West End). The next three are West (starting at Hyde Park), North (starting at Regents Park) and South (including everything south of the river). Going eastwards, we've subdivided the world into The City (EC postcodes) and The East End (E postcodes). Map references are given, where applicable, after the telephone number.

Secondly, as in England everything depends on the weather, we've divided each of the above sections into outdoor and indoor attractions. The introduction to each chapter summarises the highlights of the area concerned and tells you where you can get further local information. In addition, we've suggested sightseeing walks in most areas, to help you get your bearings and to 'join up' the various free attractions in the vicinity.

We have given the most up-to-date information available, but details change and it's always a good idea to call ahead (or look at websites, where applicable) to check opening times and any other details of particular interest. If you are making a special trip, you should always confirm the arrangements that apply over holiday periods – opening hours may be modified, of course, but there may also be special events worth knowing about.

Indexes

If you're interested in a particular type of attraction, wherever it is to be found, don't miss the indexes. There, we've given lists of all the museums, all the parks, all the galleries, and so on, to make sure you don't miss out on anything.

We hope that this book will help you to find London as fascinating a place as we continually do. And if you find something we've missed, please do write to tell us.

chard Harden   **Peter Harden**

*Londonwide
information*

Introduction

A huge amount of free information about London is there for the taking. It's very difficult to find yourself far from a public library, and you don't of course need to be a resident of the area concerned to go and browse through the newspapers, listings magazines and guide books.

The most central comprehensive resources are to be found at:

Westminster Reference Library, just by Leicester Square 35 St Martin's Street WC2, (020) 7641 4636

Victoria
160 Buckingham Palace Road SW1, (020) 7641 4636

Chelsea
Old Town Hall, King's Road SW3, (020) 7352 6056

St Pancras
opposite the railway station NW1, (020) 7974 5833

Swiss Cottage
88 Avenue Road NW3, (020) 7974 6522

Consult the telephone directory to find out where your local library is (listed under the name of the relevant borough).

Some libraries offer free internet access (if sometimes only to registered members). The most central such service is Westminster Reference Library. Bookings are taken in advance and you are limited to an hour's use at any one time. Understandably it's very popular. Bookings: (020) 7641 4636. (Times: Mon-Fri 10am-8pm, Sat 10am-5pm).

Libraries are also great places to find posters and leaflets about what's going on in an area, so if you want inspiration for free things to do close to home, your local library is almost certainly the best place to start.

Locals shouldn't overlook the tourist information offices, which often have a lot of information about events that are of just as much interest to Londoners as they are to visitors. In each of the area chapters, we've listed these offices.

The following services provide information on a pan-London basis.

London Tourist Board SW1

Victoria Station   0906 866 3344   2–4B

The main Tourist Information Centre of the LTB at Victoria Station welcomes millions of visitors every year. As a general source of free, up-to-date information about the metropolis, it's long been one of the best places in town. The LTB has some branches, which we've listed in the appropriate areas.

Call the tourist board number (listed above) for the latest recorded information although beware that this is a premium number at 60p a minute. Alternatively call 0870 240 4326 to request a free information pack which includes six different guides on shopping, restaurants, royalty, accommodation and useful telephone numbers. Or for a quicker response visit their very useful website. / Times: Jan-Feb 8am-7pm; Mar-May 8am-8pm; Jun-Sep 8am-9pm; Oct-Dec 8am-6.15pm; www.londontouristboard.com; Tube: Victoria.

Britain Visitor Centre SW1

1 Regent St   2–2C

As its name suggests, this office not far from Piccadilly Circus is a good source of information about Britain generally, as well as about London. / Times: Mon-Fri 9am-6.30pm, Sat & Sun 10am-4pm; Tube: Piccadilly Circus.

Public Transport Enquiries SW1

Windsor House, 42-50 Victoria St   (020) 7222 1234   2–4B

This 24-hour telephone service is an invaluable source of help for any queries about services run by Transport for London (which runs the Underground, London Buses, the Docklands Light Railway, River Services and Victoria Coach Station).

The Travel Information Office on the concourse of Victoria Station (opposite platform 8) is an excellent source of maps and brochures to enable you to use London's public transport efficiently. There are also TICs at: Heathrow Terminals 1, 2 and 4; and at the Terminals 1, 2, and 3 Underground stations (Mon-Sat); West Croydon, Euston; Hammersmith (Mon-Sat); Piccadilly Circus; St James's Park (Mon-Fri); Liverpool Street; Oxford Circus; Paddington (Mon-Sun).

A series of free leaflets entitled Simply London – with information on various subjects from discovering East London to shopping for food – is available from most Underground stations or from their website. / Times: 7.45am (Sun 8.45am)-7pm; www.transportforlondon.gov.uk; Tube: Victoria.

Social Action
(020) 7484 4000
Capital Radio's all-year information line, Social Action (formerly Capital Helplines), will try to answer your questions – however practical or offbeat. At various times of year, Capital also offers special helplines (numbers vary) such as revision lines (before GCSEs). One of the most popular lines is the Flatshare service (tel (020) 7484 8000). It is free to advertise a vacant room and lists are published in The Guardian *on Thu or are available free of charge, from 4pm Fri, from Capital Radio at 30 Leicester Square WC2. Listen in to 95.8 FM for details of the occasional services or try the website. / Times: helpline: Mon-Fri 9am-9pm; www.capitalfm.com.*

Newspapers

Metro
Metro is a daily free newspaper published by the company that owns the Evening Standard and Daily Mail. It can be picked up at Underground stations each weekday morning – look for the blue metal dump bins. You'll need to be quick, as they're usually all gone by 9am. In addition to general news, it has listings of events happening that day, including free or inexpensive sources of entertainment. / www.metro.co.uk..

Ms London, Girl About Town, Nine to Five, Midweek, London Monthly
A range of magazines aimed at differing sections of London's inhabitants (South Africans, Canadians, South Americans...) is available from dump bins outside principal tube and rail stations. As well as articles, listings and reviews, they often include discount vouchers for services and even the occasional offer of a free haircut.

TNT
It may not be quite as comprehensive as Time Out *(which is free only on consultation in public libraries), but TNT – the weekly magazine for expat Aussies and Kiwis – is obtainable without any charge and has quite good theatre, cinema and other event listings. It also includes details of the many free slide shows organised by the main trekking and adventure companies to publicise their holidays. There are also articles of general budget interest, too. Pick a copy up from the publication's spiritual home – outside Earl's Court tube – or from street dispensers throughout central London, including major rail and tube stations. / www.tntmagazine.com.*

Other information

Alternative Arts
(020) 7375 0441
This organisation provides a platform for various performing artists, and strives to make the arts easily accessible for the general public. Events (which range from outdoor opera performances to African dance and drama) are all free and happen in public places – Victoria Embankment Gardens WC2 and Berkeley Square W1, for example. For details of what's on during the year send an SAE to Alternative Arts, Top Studio, Bethnal Green Training Centre, Deal Street, London E1 5HZ. / www.alternativearts.co.uk.

Books
This book is a general guide, designed as an introduction to the many free delights which London has to offer. There are of course many special interests which you can pursue in London without cost, upon which there is much more information available than we are able to set out here. The following are some of the most handy books currently in print – you can also borrow them from a library – to give you more information. The best, most comprehensive, general guide is probably the Eyewitness Travel Guide *(Dorling Kindersley, 2001), with listings, pictures and descriptions of galleries, museums, walks and architecture. Other guides of note include those published by Fodor's, Rough Guides and Lonely Planet.* Museums and Galleries of London *(Abigail Willis, 2001) provides an intelligent overview of its subject, without going into so much detail as to put off the general reader.* London Markets *(Phil Harris, 2002) tells you everything you might want to know about the capital's colourful street life. The* Time Out Book of London Walks *(Andrew White, 2001) provides an interesting collection of intellectual, cultural and historical peregrinations.*

The City, its churches and architecture
The churches of the City (many by Wren) are among London's greatest architectural treasures. A leaflet, available from the City of London Information Centre (see City section), actually lists all buildings of historical and architectural interest within the Square Mile. Opening times, maps, the nearest tube stations and suggested walking routes are included, as well as a brief history of the City and sketches of the buildings described.

Disabled access
There are several services which are very helpful for disabled people who are exploring London.

General queries relating in any way to travel for the disabled and elderly (and including information about hire of vehicles) can be addressed to Tripscope (The Vassall Centre, Gill Avenue, Bristol BS16 2QQ; 0845 758 5641). Transport for London offers a free guide to public transport, available from TfL Access & Mobility (tel: (020) 7941 4600).

Londonwide information

To check out the details of the access arrangements for any place of entertainment or tourist attraction in London you can call Artsline (54 Chalton Street, London NW1 1HS; (020) 7388 2227). Artsline also distributes a range of access guides, including some to tourist attractions (nominal charge). Also worth consulting is www.theatre-access.co.uk, which holds details on disabled access to the capital's theatres. For those interested in finding physical activities, The British Sports Association for the Disabled also has a useful website – www.disabilitysports.org.uk, where one can find information on trampolining and swimming groups, amongst others.

Galleries
London remains one of the great centres of the international market in pictures and objets d'art. Much of the business is conducted through galleries to which the public has free access.

We can't lead you to the changing artistic attractions of the capital, as many of the most interesting commercial shows last for only a month or so. However, help is at hand in the form of an excellent monthly publication – Galleries – of which you can obtain a copy, gratis, from almost any commercial art gallery. Its handy format contains a wealth of information, helpfully organised into areas (with maps) and indexed in every way you could possibly want (including by artist and type of work). It also contains short but interesting articles on many of the forthcoming attractions. Many other publications, such as Time Out, also provide comprehensive listings.

You could easily spend a week just exploring London's commercial galleries. As a starting point, the greatest concentrations are found around Cork Street, Bruton Street and Old Bond Street W1, and in St James's SW1. There are also clusters of galleries around the junction of Portobello Road and Westbourne Grove W11 and in Walton Street SW3. Those in search of more 'alternative' displays should head north or east, to Camden, Islington and Hoxton, and nowadays even beyond.

The great auction houses are a fascinating part of the art world – details are given in the Central section.

The Internet
There are dedicated internet shops, such as easyInternetcafé, which charge a fairly small hourly rate for their services. However, the savvy traveller should keep an eye out for free opportunities to browse the web. Some libraries and museums, for example, offer free internet access.

We have listed websites with entries in this guide where possible. Some useful general websites for visitors include: www.londontown.com (from the London Tourist Board) and www.streetmap.co.uk (maps to help you find your way around).

Many of the attractions and buildings listed here are cared for by one of two national heritage bodies, English Heritage (www.english-heritage.org.uk) and The National Trust (www.nationaltrust.org.uk). Their websites contain further information on the sites and attractions for which they are responsible.

London Farmers' Markets N1
PO Box 37363   (020) 7704 9659
Farmers markets offer London consumers the opportunity to buy food direct from the grower or producer – strict guidelines ensure that no one can sell another farmer's produce, and that all goods are produced within 100 miles of London. (London's most famous foodie destination, Borough Market, see page 106, does not come under this category.) Therefore, expect to see only fresh, seasonal (sometimes organic) produce at these lively markets – the website is the most accurate way to find the times and location of your nearest market, and even gives a calendar of what fruit and vegetables you can expect to find every month. Other produce might include wine, bread, cheeses, honey and fish – stalls may even offer tasters!
/ Times: vary; www.lfm.org.uk.

London Lesbian & Gay Switchboard
(020) 7837 7324
This voluntary organisation offers a 24-hour information, support and advice helpline to lesbians and gay men. (Other sources of information include the free magazines and newspapers available in most gay bars.) / www.queery.org.uk.

Museums
The 24 Hour Museum is a charitable organisation funded by the Department of Culture, Media & Sport – it aims to promote British museums and the facilities they offer. The website (www.24hourmuseum.org.uk) provides information on current exhibitions and an online magazine, and has links to museums' own websites (where applicable). Not all of the museums listed are free. Events taking place in Museums and Galleries Month (usually in May each year) are listed on this site.

Parks

The myriad parks and open spaces of London are managed by various organisations. For individual parks listed, detailed information is provided with the appropriate entry (see the index on page 169).

Further information about Royal Parks is to be found at www.royalparks.gov.uk. The site covers comprehensive historical detail and forthcoming events in the 5,000 acres of London parkland owned by the Crown.

The Corporation of London (www.cityoflondon.gov.uk) manages over 10,000 acres of green space, woodland and parks

Londonwide information

(150 sites in the Square Mile alone, as well as Queen's Park, Epping Forest and Hampstead Heath). Call (020) 8472 3584 for a leaflet on the City.

Transport for London SW1
Windsor House, 42-50 Victoria St   (020) 7941 4500
Transport for London is the integrated body responsible for the capital's transport system set up by Mayor Ken to implement his strategy for the capital. They produce some very useful leaflets on activities in London including cycle maps, five suggested walks, information on other outdoor activities, guides to markets and so on. These can be ordered by ringing the number given, or from the website. / www.londontransport.co.uk.

Walks
One of the very best – and completely free – ways to get to know London is to walk. The bus routes mentioned in the introduction are an excellent way of connecting areas, and 'seeing the sights', but there is no match for being able to nip down intriguing alleys, investigate churches, visit urban parks, wander along canals, pop into pubs or just meander at will. Some of the books we have recommended offer interesting walks with various themes, and we have suggested walks of our own at the front of each geographical section in this book. In addition, the Green Chain Walk (see South) links many of south London's parks and open spaces.

Another excellent source of information and walk routes is the London Walking Forum (www.londonwalking.com), a partnership of organisations in and around London that have an interest in or responsibility for walking. Amongst other projects and footpath improvements made since the forum was established in 1990, a 150 mile (240 km) circular walk through the best of outer London's countryside, has been created. It is broken into 24 manageable sections, all conveniently connected to public transport.

Other activities

Bus Tours
If, as we assume, you already have a Travelcard, you can explore London from the best possible vantage point – the upper platform of a double-decker bus – at no cost. This form of tour has the virtue that you can hop on and hop off to your heart's content. If you find there are so many things to do you don't have time to finish your planned circuit, it hardly matters.

With one of Transport for London's free bus guides, you can plan your own tour, but there are two routes which are particularly suitable for a general orientation. The number 11 takes you on a great East-West tour of London, and includes many of the major sights. Start your trip at a stop in Chelsea's fashionable King's Road and ride through Victoria to Westminster Abbey.

This would be a good place to break the journey and to walk a short way – through Parliament Square, and down Whitehall to look at 10 Downing Street and the Cenotaph. Get back on the bus at the newly-revamped Trafalgar Square – having admired Nelson's Column and, if time permits, visited the National Gallery. Travel down the Strand and Fleet Street, and end at St Paul's Cathedral.

The number 15 (pick it up at Paddington, Edgware Road, Oxford Street or Regent Street) shares the Trafalgar Square to St Paul's section with the number 11 (so you can change at any point between the two). However, the 15 continues on into the City enabling you to see the Monument, Tower Bridge and the Tower of London. Travel on this route on a Sunday morning and you might press on to Aldgate, for Petticoat Lane market.
/ www.londontransport.co.uk/buses.

Courts

If you have half a day to kill, you might find it interesting, and perhaps amusing, to spend it in court. There are three types of court which will be within easy reach of most parts of London – Magistrates, Crown and County Courts.

All human life passes through London's magistrates courts, where the highest and the lowest appear to explain why they have (or have not) committed minor criminal offences, from drunkenness to speeding. Sometimes it will be pretty humdrum stuff (if not without human interest), but if you hit lucky, you may experience a real trial, probably not lasting more than a day, where the question "did he (or she) do it?" is of more than academic interest, especially to the person in the dock.

In the Crown courts, the more serious crimes – all the way up to murder – are tried by a bewigged judge and a jury. The disadvantage for the casual visitor is that most trials go on for several days, so inevitably you will see only a fraction of the proceedings. By far the most interesting theatre is to be found when a witness (especially the defendant) is being cross-examined by the opposing side's counsel. The Old Bailey (see The City) is London's senior Crown court.

County Courts resolve civil disputes (such as claims for damages, perhaps arising from a motor accident, or unpaid debts). Again, cross-examination is generally by far the most gripping part of a trial. The most important civil trials take place at the Royal Courts of Justice (see The City).

For the address of your local court, consult the telephone directory. Courts generally sit between 10am and 4.30pm. Children under 16 are not usually admitted into the public galleries. / www.courtservice.gov.uk.

Londonwide information

Fire Stations
It may be possible to organise a visit to your local fire brigade.
Write to the Commander at your nearest station.

Friday Night Skate
"Weekly (weather permitting) marshalled skating tour of
London, accompanied by a portable sound system", 7.30pm-
9.30pm - meet at Duke of Wellington Arch, Hyde Park Corner.
Visit the website for full details. / www.citiskate.com.

London Cyclist
Try your local library for the bi-monthly magazine of the very
active London Cycling Campaign (tel (020) 7928 7220, Mon-
Fri 10am-5pm). Every issue has details of social, weekend
rides, and in summer, and during Bike week (second week in
June), evening and early morning rides. All rides are guided and
free (although some may involve train journeys).

Volunteers at bi-monthly 'stuffing' evenings (putting copies of
London Cyclist into envelopes ready for posting) are rewarded
with free vegetarian food and the chance to swap details of
potholes and near-misses with a range of like-minded people.
During Bike Week there are several cyclists' breakfasts – more
free grub if you can get up early enough to pedal off and join
in! / www.lcc.org.uk.

London Wildlife Trust SE1
Harling House, 47-51 Great Suffolk St   (020) 7261 0447
The Trust's aim is to sustain and enhance London's wildlife
habitats, and to this end it manages 57 nature reserves – a
free map of locations is available. Each year, more than 600
free indoor and outdoor events, classes and volunteer
opportunities are organised – from bat walks to wild flower
talks. Call the number given to obtain information packs and
factsheets, as well as details and locations of volunteer contacts
throughout London. / Times: Mon-Fri 9.30am-5.30pm;
www.wildlondon.org.uk.

Royal Society of Arts* WC2
8 John Adam St   (020) 7930 5115   2–2C
The Royal Society for the Encouragement of Arts,
Manufactures and Commerce (to give it its full name) is
located just off the Strand, in a fine house that was designed
for the Society by Robert Adam in the 1770s. It is open to the
public on the first Sunday of each month and at Christmas
provides a free lecture for children. (A paid-for programme of
around 40 lectures a year takes place between October and
April. Lectures are primarily aimed at members, but non-
members are welcome to attend if they apply in advance for a
ticket – via the website or by phone. The range of subjects is
wide: for example 'A future for Rail Transport', or 'The balance
of Nature, Land Management and Conservation'.) / Times: first
Sunday of every month (except Jan) from 10am-1pm; www.rsa.org.uk;
Tube: Embankment, Charing Cross.

Annual timetable

Barely a month goes by in London without some great event happening which can provide a good focus for a day out, especially with children in tow. The major events which happen on an annual basis are as follows.

January

London Parade
0900 525 2020 (recorded information)
The New Year starts with a bang as an American-style family event takes place on the first day of the year. Hundreds of thousands of people turn out to see the big parade, with 6,000 majorettes (flown in from the States), clowns, floats and dance displays. It starts from Parliament Square at noon and the final band reaches Berkeley Square in Mayfair around 3pm. The procession (for which Whitehall or Piccadilly offers the best vantage point) consists of marching bands, floats and horse-drawn carriages, in which ride the Archbishop and Lord Mayor of Westminster and mayors of all the London boroughs (but not, of course, the fiercely independent City).
/ www.londonparade.co.uk; Tube: Westminster, St James's Park, Green Park.

Chinese New Year
In late January or early February, Chinatown celebrates the Chinese New Year with noisy, colourful parades (including the famous papier mâché dragons), which last most of the day (11am-6.30pm). The whole area (around Gerrard Street W1) is brightly decorated for the event. / Tube: Leicester Square.

London International Mime Festival*
(020) 7637 5661
The festival aims to be a showcase for the best international visual theatre, at several central London venues, over a 16 day period each January. Events take place at the Royal Festival Hall, The Barbican, BAC and the ICA and, although most require the purchase of a ticket, some are free (ring or check the website for details). Artforms include mime, circus, puppetry, acrobatics and performance art. / www.mimefest.co.uk.

February

Pancake Day Races
Covent Garden WC2/ Spitalfields Market E1
(020) 7375 0441 (Alternative Arts)
Shrove Tuesday ('Pancake Day') sees traditional races between pancake-tossing relay-teams at Spitalfields (12.30pm).
/ Tube: Liverpool Street.

Events

March

Head of the River Race
(01932) 220401
The Oxford and Cambridge Boat Race may be more famous, but, for the casual observer, the Head of the River Race, rowed on a Saturday in March from Mortlake to Putney, is probably more interesting to watch. The sheer number of crews (usually over 400) means that the colourful procession of eight-oared boats (which are set off 10 seconds apart) takes well over an hour. Being a timed race, it does have the disadvantage that no one knows who has won until it's all over. Best vantage points are as for the Boat Race (below), but those in the know go to Chiswick Bridge to watch the pre-race marshalling of hundreds of boats in a confined stretch of the river. Start times vary according to the tides. / www.horr.co.uk; Tube: Putney Bridge; Picnic area.

Oxford & Cambridge Boat Race
It may be an arcane and thoroughly English way of spending an afternoon, but the world's most famous boat race, between Oxford and Cambridge University Boat Clubs, continues to exercise an extraordinary grip on the popular imagination. Tens of thousands of people turn out every year to snatch a passing glimpse of an 18-minute race (first rowed on the Thames in 1830) which, from a practical point of view, is much better watched on television. The best vantage points for the four-mile race from Putney to Mortlake are generally held to be at the half-way point (Hammersmith) or at the finish – but you don't get much of a view anywhere and the real point is not really the race but the atmosphere. Take a picnic and – if you want to know who's won – a radio. / www.theboatrace.org; Tube: Hammersmith, Putney Bridge.

April

Flora London Marathon
(020) 7620 4117
The London Marathon, first run in 1981, has grown into a huge event which attracts more than 40,000 runners and over half a million spectators annually. Its sheer scale and spectacle makes it a good family day out. Over half of the runners are taking part for charity (and collectively raise over £30 million). Many run in costume, and you may see some famous faces. The course of just over 26 miles begins (around 9am) in Greenwich Park and ends (having taken a circuitous route) outside Buckingham Palace. The leading runners take a little over two hours to complete the course, but the stragglers make it practically an all-day event. / www.london-marathon.co.uk.

Kite Festival SE3
Streatham Common
Around Easter (often on the Monday) each year sees London's leading annual kite festival – a good spectacle whether you're interested in kite-flying or not. It used to be in Blackheath, but has now moved here. / www.kitecalendar.co.uk; BR: Blackheath.

May

Canalway Cavalcade W9
Pool of Little Venice, Paddington   (0192) 371 1114
Watercrafts of all types take part in the colourful boat rally organised by the Inland Waterways Association. In conjunction, this lively, family event boasts live music, Morris dancing, a teddy bears picnic, boat trips and waterway-related trade and craft stalls. An evening highlight is the illuminated boat procession which takes place on the Sunday. / Times: May Day bank hol weekend, 10am-6pm & Sun eve; www.waterways.org.uk; Tube: Warwick Avenue.

Covent Garden Flower Festival WC2
The Piazza   (020) 7836 9136
Taking place annually in the last week of June in this former fruit and veg market, the Festival (begun in 1997) presents innovative and contemporary flower displays and garden installations combined with theatrical productions and promotions. It focuses on new designs, products and services and is aimed particularly at the urban gardener. The festival has its own catwalk show called Fashion Flowers, in which floral accessories and even complete outfits are made solely of flowers. The main attraction is the performance garden, a large-scale installation in front of St Paul's Church, offering a platform for street theatre, opera, music and dance. There are also displays and promotions in the Seven Dials area, a short stroll north of Covent Garden piazza. / Tube: Covent Garden, Leicester Square.

Coin Street Festival SE1
Gabriel's Wharf, Bernie Spain Gardens, Oxo Tower Wharf
(020) 7928 0960
A popular and growing annual event that runs from mid-June to September, and which celebrates the many cultures and interests of the people who live, work in, or visit the capital. Highlights are live music and street performances – from French street theatre to African storytelling – and there are many activities for children, including workshops and competitions. Almost every weekend there is a day of events, all of which are free, usually around a particular theme – call for a leaflet. / www.coinstreetfestival.org; Tube: Waterloo, Blackfriars, Southwark.

May Fayre & Puppet Festival WC2
St Paul's Church & Gardens, Bedford St
(020) 7375 0441 (Alternative Arts)
This all-day event, which takes place on the Sunday nearest to 9 May, celebrates the art of puppetry, with Punch and Judy performers from all over the country. There's a parade at 10.30am and a service in St Paul's Church, from 11.30am. / Times: 10.30am-5.30pm; www.alternativearts.co.uk; Tube: Covent Garden, Leicester Square.

Events

Museums & Galleries Month*
*During May, around 1400 museums and galleries in the
capital and across the country – including many of the free
institutions listed in this book – put on special events. (This
event was previously called Museums Week.) Full details
appear in the Radio Times, local newspapers and on the
website. / www.museumsweek.org.uk.*

June

Vauxhall Festival
(020) 7793 0263 (Vauxhall St Peter's Heritage Centre)
*Local organisations and individuals take the stage at Vauxhall
St Peter's Heritage Centre for a variety of arts and community
events, highlighting the local contemporary arts scene. The last
day is an all-day outdoor music festival.*

City of London Festival* EC2
Bishopsgate Hall, 230 Bishopsgate   (020) 7377 0540
*In late June/early July, the City enjoys an explosion of music. If
you're looking for free events, seek out the world music series
which takes place on weekday lunchtimes at venues throughout
the Square Mile – workers and tourists alike are entertained by
street theatre and dance, jazz, Latin and brass bands. There is
almost invariably a charge for the evening events. For full
listings and timetables, see the website. / www.colf.org.*

Devizes to Westminster International Canoe Race
*Often referred to as the 'Canoeist's Everest', this claims to be
the world's toughest canoe race, lasting for three days and 125
miles (the course must be completed in under 100 hours). It
has been raced every Easter since 1948, along the Kennet and
Avon Canal to Reading, where it enters the Thames. You can
watch the end of the race, at Westminster Bridge (usually
around 9am on Mon morning) from the relative comfort of the
Embankment. / www.dwrace.org.uk.*

Henley Royal Regatta*
(01491) 572153, tourist information (01491) 578034
*Henley, established in 1839, is the world's oldest major rowing
regatta. It takes place in late June/early July (the final Sunday is
always the 27th Sunday of the year). Even if you've never been
in a rowing boat in your life, and even if you don't know anyone
who is a member of one of the enclosures, it's still one of the
most enjoyable events of the 'Season' and manages, to an
extraordinary extent, to maintain something of the atmosphere
of an Edwardian garden party. Take a picnic, arrive early, and
find a good viewpoint along the towpath – all but the last third
of a mile or so of the course is open to the public, and at many
points you can hear the commentary. The event lasts from
Wednesday to Sunday – it's much less crowded on the
weekdays. / www.hrr.co.uk; BR: Henley on Thames.*

Events

Regular events

Ceremony of the Keys EC3
Tower of London   (020) 7709 0765
In accordance with seven centuries of tradition, the Tower of London (home, of course, to the Crown Jewels) is secured for the night with a 10 minute ceremony. Anyone can apply for a ticket to attend, but you need to do so in writing enclosing an SAE (Ceremony of the Keys, The Operations Department, HM Tower of London, London EC3N 4AB) stating the names and addresses of those in your group and the date you would like to attend, giving at least two months' notice. / Times: nightly at 9.30pm; www.tower-of-london.com/traditions; Tube: Tower Hill.

Changing the Guard (Buckingham Palace) SW1
The changing of the sentries at Buckingham Palace is famous around the world. The new guard leaves Wellington Barracks three minutes before the change, and, preceded by a band, marches down Birdcage Walk to the palace. The ceremony lasts 40 minutes, and takes place inside the railings of the palace itself. The event is subject to cancellation in very bad weather or during state visits. In conjunction with this event, the St. James's Palace detachment of the Queen's Guard marches to Buckingham Palace at 11.15am and back to St. James's Palace at 12.10pm. / Times: Apr-Oct, daily at 11.30am; Nov-Mar, every other day; www.londontown.com; Tube: Green Park.

Changing the Guard (Horse Guards) SW1
Horse Guards Parade
In a daily burst of pageantry, a mounted guard leaves Hyde Park Barracks at 10.28am (Sun 9.28am) and proceeds, via Hyde Park Corner and Constitution Hill, to arrive at Horse Guards Parade at 11am (Sun 10am), where the guard is changed. The splendidly attired mounted guardsmen making their way through Hyde Park offers what is probably London's most romantic sight. / Times: daily at 11am, Sun 10am; www.londontown.com; Tube: Hyde Park Corner, St James's Park.

Gun Salutes
One of the most striking sights in London is the gun salutes which hail royal and state events. These take place in Green, St James's or Hyde Park (12 noon) and at the Tower of London (1pm) on the following dates (or, if a Sunday, the next day): 6 February (Accession Day); 21 April (the Queen's birthday); 2 June (Coronation Day); and 10 June (the Duke of Edinburgh's birthday). Salutes also mark state visits (usually in May and October), Trooping the Colour (June) and the State Opening of Parliament (October or November). Details of these and other events in the Royal Parks are given in the Summer Entertainment Programme available with an A5 SAE from the Old Police House, Hyde Park, London W2 2UH (tel (020) 7298 2000). / www.royalparks.co.uk; Tube: Hyde Park Corner, Tower Hill.

Mardi Gras*

London's major lesbian and gay festival takes place in late June/early July. The event (for which there is a charge) usually includes an impressive line-up of world-renowned musical artists, and follows a colourful street march and float parade (actually organised by Pride, who used to run the whole event) which is free for all to watch. The parade usually starts from Hyde Park Corner at noon; check newspapers or the website for the precise route. / www.londonmardigras.com.

Spitalfields Summer Festival* E1

75 Brushfield St   Hotline (020) 7377 1362

Spitalfields plays host to yearly music festivals – in summer and another one just before Christmas. The festivals hold a varied programme of lunchtime and evening concerts of music from c15 to contemporary. There are also exhibitions and a fringe festival, including arts events, comedy and circus performances. Call or check the website for further details.
/ www.spitalfieldsfestival.org.uk; Tube: Shoreditch, Liverpool Street, Aldgate East.

Stokefest* N16

Box Office, c/o Stoke Newington Library, Stoke Newington Church St   (020) 8356 6411

Previously known as the Stoke Newington Festival, some kind of future now seems assured for the event (which ceased trading in 2002). It's final future shape is still unclear – historically this annual independent arts festival has stretched across four weekends in June and showcased Hackney-based artists, performers and musicians. Many events, including poetry readings, walks and listening to the dawn chorus, have been free. Visual arts events, including installations and photographic exhibitions, used to take place in unusual settings including Abney Park Cemetery (see also). / www.stokenewingtonfestival.co.uk; BR: Stoke Newington or 73 bus.

Trooping the Colour*

(020) 7930 4466

A Saturday in early June sees the celebration of the Queen's Official Birthday, when she inspects an elaborate military display at Horse Guards Parade SW1. At 1pm, after her return to Buckingham Palace, there is an RAF flypast down the Mall.

There is a charge to attend the event itself (although, of course, you can watch the procession down the Mall), but tickets for the first rehearsal (The Major General's Review) are free, (two or three Saturdays before), and (as for the main event) are allocated by ballot. Apply in January or February, with an SAE, to Brigade Major (Trooping the Colour), Headquarters, Household Division, Horse Guards, Whitehall London SW1A 2AX. Check newspapers or www.londontown.com for times and dates. / Tube: St James's Park.

Events

Croydon Forestry Country Show
Selsdon Wood, Old Farleigh Rd   (020) 8253 1009
A family day out in the countryside. Features have included falconry displays, classic cars, pony rides, ancient (but working) farm machinery and rare breeds of farm animals. Refreshments are also in copious supply. / Times: Mid August;Sat-Sun 10.00am-5.00pm approx; www.croydon.gov.uk; BR: East Croydon & then 64 bus to Selsdon & then free shuttle to show ground; Café, Picnic area.

Croydon Summer Festival*, Surrey
(020) 8253 1030
Previously known as the Croydon Jazz Week (which was well-known for traditional jazz), the arts festival now encompasses a wide range of live music, including street performance, Caribbean and Latin, as well as jazz. A highlight is the Croydon Mela, London's second largest Asian music festival. A full brochure of events is available approximately two months prior to the festival, which lasts for two weeks in July / www.croydon.gov.uk/summerfestival; Café.

Dogget's Coat & Badge Race
The oldest event in British sport, this sculling race takes place from Chelsea to London Bridge (or the Coat and Badge pub, to be precise). It was in 1751 that Thomas Dogget, an Irish actor and comedian, funded the first race, to commemorate the accession of George I. It was originally restricted to 'professional watermen' only, but the rules have been relaxed to permit amateurs in recent years.

Ealing Countryside Weekend
Berkeley Fields, opposite Ballot Box pub, Horsenden Ln North, Greenford   (020) 8758 5916
Cancelled for 2003 but possibly to be re-launched in 2004: this is one of the biggest waterside events in London. Attractions in the past have included dancing, international food stalls, farm activities, a craft village and environmental displays. / Times: Sat 12pm-10pm, Sun 11am-8pm; www.ealing.gov.uk; Tube: Greenford, Perivale.

Ealing Summer*
(020) 8825 5000
Ealing's annual festival, now called Ealing Summer, is a month-long series of events in the parks and streets around Ealing. Some events are ticket only but of the free events, entertainments include a Blues party in Walpole Park and a Street Arts Festival in central and west Ealing. Other events (which may charge an entrance fee) include a comedy festival, the Ealing Film Festival and a classical concert in Gunnersbury Park – check the website or call for the events timetable. The festival is followed by the Ealing Jazz Festival (see also). / www.ealing.gov.uk/events; Tube: Ealing Broadway.

Greenwich & Docklands International Festival*
(020) 8305 1818
This multi-arts extravaganza (which takes place every July) now spans both banks of the Thames (and much of east London). Many of the attractions are free and include opening and closing night pyrotechnics, open-air music and dance performances. For details, you can visit the website or ring the festival hotline. / www.festival.org; Tube: Greenwich, Woolwich (DLR).

Hillingdon Borough Carnival
Hayes, Middx   (01895) 250029
Every year the second Saturday in July sees the streets of Hayes erupt with floats and crowds. Up to 20 floats, followed by marching bands, lead the way from Pump Lane at 12.30pm, to Barra Hall Park. Here you will find a funfair, Punch and Judy shows, clowns, stalls, pony rides, live music, stilt-walking, gladiators and impersonators. / www.hillingdon.gov.uk; BR: Hayes and Harlington.

Swan Upping
(020) 7236 1863
All the swans on the Thames between London Bridge and Henley belong to the Queen or one of two City livery companies: the Dyers and the Vintners. This cosy three-way arrangement has been in place since 1510. Each year, it is necessary to mark the cygnets to show to whom they belong (which depends on who owns their parents). This task is carried out every 3rd week of July, by a procession of six 'Thames Skiffs' (rowed by colourfully-uniformed oarsmen), which takes a week to progress from Sunbury to Abingdon Bridge. When swans are spotted, the traditional cry of "All-up" is raised, and they are coralled by three skiffs, one staffed by each of the potential owners, in preparation for identification and marking. The swans, it seems, do not always come quietly. If you want to know when and where you can witness this extraordinary ritual, call the Vintners on the number given. Traditionally, swans were marked by nicking their bills, but they are now ringed instead – in deference to tradition, the practice is, of course, known as 'nicking'. / www.royal.gov.uk.

August

Ealing Jazz Festival
(020) 8825 5000
Started in 1985, the 'friendly festival' – so-called because of its family atmosphere – claims to be the largest free jazz festival in Britain (some 50,000 people visit over its course). Lunchtime and evening concerts are led by musicians playing fusion, Latin and modern jazz on a stage in Walpole Park. There are also a variety of activities organised for children during the day. The festival usually takes place at the end of July/beginning of August. (Taking place alongside it is an International Food Fair.) / www.ealing.gov.uk/events; Tube: Ealing Broadway.

Events

Notting Hill Carnival

*The August bank holiday sees the largest street party in Europe
– over a million people attending a musical celebration of Afro-
Caribbean culture. The carnival is centred around the northern
parts of the Portobello Road. Sunday sees the Children's
Carnival Day, while the main procession of floats takes place
on Monday. There is music for all tastes, including reggae, jazz,
hip-hop and house. The whole event is certainly impressive in
its sheer scale and vitality, but this may make it seem rather
daunting to some people. All the common-sense rules of
attending such a large and crowded occasion apply – don't
drive there, keep hold of children, carry as little money as
possible, and don't hang around once the daytime festivities are
over. Leave your English reserve at home, and the music and
atmosphere might well transport you to the Caribbean!*
/ www.nhct.net.uk; Tube: Notting Hill Gate, Ladbroke Grove.

September

Thames Festival

Victoria Embankment and South Bank by OXO Tower
(020) 7928 8998
*From Frost Fairs to GLC Thames Days, London's river has long
been a natural focal point for pageantry and celebrations. The
Thames Festival begins from Victoria Embankment, with a
spectacular processional of over 2500 illuminated sculptures
and lanterns, representing the effort of school children and
community groups throughout London. The procession ends at
the Royal National Theatre with a magnificent fireworks display
on the river. Call the Thames Festival Trust for details.*
/ Times: -2nd or 3rd weekend in September; Sat-Sun; www.thamesfestival.org;
Tube: Waterloo, Southwark, Blackfriars; Café.

Angel Canal Festival N1

City Road Basin, Regent's Canal, off Wharf Rd
(020) 7267 9100
*This annual community festival celebrates the Regent's Canal in
Islington, and is based around City Road Lock and Basin.
Always held on the first Sunday in September, the festival
features a variety of stalls, a fun-fair, music, boat trips and a
regatta.* / Times: 11.30am-5.30pm; Tube: Angel.

Great River Race

c/o Stuart Wolff (020) 8398 9057
*This ever more popular event (which takes place in September)
has all the ingredients of a Great British Success Story. For a
start, the idea behind it is completely – inspiringly – batty. Take
more than 250 oared boats (rule: no racing-boats allowed),
devise a handicapping system (which allows some boats to
start 100 minutes before others) and set them off (down a
tidal river) on a 22-mile journey from Ham House in Richmond
to Island Gardens on the Isle of Dogs. The event attracts every
type of boat (from Chinese dragon boats to Hawaiian war
canoes) and rowers and paddlers of all ages and of every
degree of seriousness, from all over the world.*

It's a wonderful spectacle, and one which can be viewed from any London bank of the Thames, though the greatest excitement is of course at the start, at Richmond, (3.30pm) and the finish: best viewing by the Cutty Sark, in Greenwich (6.45pm). / www.greatriverrace.co.uk; Tube: choice of 12 riverside stations between Richmond and Island Gardens (DLR).

Heritage Open Days
(020) 7930 0914
The Civic Trust co-ordinates an annual exercise which allows the public to see, for free, buildings of historic or architectural interest that are usually closed to general enquirers. The celebration takes place in the second weekend of September and highlights various properties, from windmills to music halls, throughout England. For details of the buildings that will be open, write to Heritage Open Day, Civic Trust, 17 Carlton House Terrace, London SW1Y 5AW, enclosing six second-class stamps or check the website. / www.heritageopendays.org.uk.

London Open House
0900 1600 061
Heritage Open Day (see above) is a national event. The London equivalent takes place a week later. On these dates the public can gain free admittance to all types of buildings, from cinemas and colleges to theatres, even perhaps a former mortuary, which are not normally accessible. Over 500 buildings are open to the public for free. There are also walks, exhibitions and lectures. The idea is to celebrate London's wealth of architecture, to promote public awareness of architecture and the built environment and to encourage civic pride. In addition, there are building tours and activities specifically designed for children. For details, look for leaflets in galleries around town or, for a comprehensive directory of buildings involved in the scheme, send an A5 envelope with 41p in stamps on it and £2 in stamps inside, a couple of months in advance, to: London Open House, PO Box 25361, London NW5 1GY. / www.londonopenhouse.org.

National Trust Free Entry Day
0870 609 5380
There's generally a charge to enter National Trust properties (except for members), but on one day a year many properties are open free of charge (there is no fixed day as it's up to the individual properties when they decide to open for free). Needless to say, if you value tranquillity, this is probably not the best time to go. The Trust does not generally advertise the dates — for fear of attracting crowds of people who can perfectly well afford to pay — so you'll have to keep your ear to the ground. / www.nationaltrust.org.uk.

Events

Raising of the Thames Barrier SE18
Unity Way   (020) 8854 1373

Canute was wrong – you can hold back the tide, but only by spending half a billion pounds on a great river barrier, designed to protect central London from the ever-growing risk of flooding. The Thames Barrier (see also, South London) is a miracle of modern engineering (completed in 1982). Once a year (usually in September or October) there is an all-day test and the massive steel gates are either raised or dropped against the high tide. There are also tests each month, but these take place as early in the morning as tides permit and (because it involves closing a working river) for as short a period as possible. Call the Thames Barrier Information and Learning Centre for details. / Times: Apr-Sep 10.30am-4.30pm, Sep-Mar 11am-3.30pm; www.environment-agency.gov.uk; BR: Charlton; Café.

October

Diwali
Funfairs and fireworks take place in Ealing and Hounslow in October to mark one of the largest festivals celebrating Hindus, Sikhs and Jains. Check press for details. Local councils often organise festivals.

Punch & Judy Festival WC2
Covent Garden   (020) 7836 9136

The first Sunday of October sees a plethora of Punch and Judy shows, and their continental equivalents – Polichinelle (France), Kasper (Germany) and Pulcinella (Italy). / Tube: Leicester Square.

Southwark Festival*
(020) 7403 7400

Making full use of Southwark's river frontage (which stretches from Tower Bridge to the Millennium footbridge) and unusual venues (including the chapel of Guy's Hospital), the festival's fortnight of events ranges from street theatre and concerts in Southwark Cathedral to historical lectures about the area's past inhabitants, a food fair in Borough Market and contemporary art in Tate Modern. Much of the programme is free (both indoor and outdoor events); call or check the website for other events held earlier in the year. / www.southwarkfestival.org.uk; Tube: Southwark, London Bridge, Borough.

State Opening of Parliament
If you want to see the Queen wearing a crown and riding in a gilded coach, the only annual opportunity to do so is the State Opening of Parliament (sometimes in Oct, usually Nov). Her Majesty rides from Buckingham Palace to Westminster to deliver the Queen's Speech (which sets out the Government's legislative plans for the forthcoming year, and is, in fact, written by the Prime Minister) and then returns to her palace. There are accompanying gun salutes at Green Park and the Tower of London. As an event, it's not hugely well attended, and offers possibly the best 'royal-watching' opportunity of the year. / www.parliament.uk/parliament/guide/maopen.htm; Tube: Westminster.

Trafalgar Day Parade WC2
Trafalgar Sq
A commemoration service for Nelson's 1805 victory at Trafalgar takes place on the nearest Sunday to 21 October. Wreaths are laid at Nelson's Column by over 500 Sea Cadets.
/ Tube: Leicester Square, Charing Cross.

November

RAC London to Brighton Veteran Car Run
Saturday 14 November 1896 was a great day in the history of British motoring – for the first time it was legal to proceed at more than 4mph and without being preceded by a man with a red flag (the new speed limit was set at a staggering 14mph). Ever since (war years excepted), horseless carriages have taken part in an annual celebration of automobile 'Emancipation'. The spectacle now attracts over a million spectators each year. The Run – it is NOT a race – takes place on the first Sunday in November, leaving Hyde Park at 7.30am, and progressing via Westminster (7.35am) and Lambeth Town Hall (7.45am) to Madeira Drive, Brighton, where the frontrunners arrive around 10.30am. Only cars built before 1905 are eligible to take part, and competitors come from all over the world.
/ www.vccofgb.co.uk/lontobri/index.htm; Tube: Hyde Park Corner.

Fireworks Night
The annual remembrance of the failure of the Gunpowder Plot (when Guy Fawkes and his merry men attempted, in 1605, to blow up monarch, lords and commoners assembled at Westminster) is celebrated with a large number of bonfire and firework parties of all sizes all over London. Parties take place on November 5 and, if it falls mid-week, the weekends before and after. The larger events are widely advertised on posters and in local newspapers.

Lord Mayor's Show
The Lord Mayor's Show has taken place – plague permitting – in some form in most years since 1215. It celebrates the annual presentation of the new Lord Mayor of London to the Queen's Justices. This formerly took place at Westminster, but now involves a rather shorter journey to the Royal Courts of Justice in the Strand. The show takes place on the second Saturday of November, and begins at the Guildhall at 11am with a one-and-a-half-mile long procession, which includes 200 horses, 60 floats, 20 bands and about 6,000 people. The centrepiece of the procession is the Lord Mayor's gilded, c18 coach (housed for the rest of the year in the Museum of London, see also), pulled by six shire horses. This is a great traditional Londoners' day out – a whole day's entertainment is provided, ending with a firework display over the Thames – and about a half of a million people attend annually. Many City attractions, generally closed at weekends, open on the day of the show. / www.lordmayorsshow.org; Tube: Bank.

Events

Remembrance Sunday SW1
Whitehall
The Sunday nearest to 11 November sees the most sober, and the most moving, large-scale event of the year. Just after 11am, the Queen and representatives of the government and the Commonwealth lay wreaths of Flanders poppies on the Cenotaph to commemorate those who gave their lives in war. After the short service, the tone becomes a little lighter as the veterans march past. / Tube: Embankment, Charing Cross, Westminster.

December

Christmas Lights
The heartland of London's shopping – Oxford Street, Regent Street and Bond Street – puts on a good-enough festive show (though by international standards it would be difficult to describe the illuminations as a 'must-do' experience). Carnaby Street also joins in, usually with some fairly avant-garde variations on the festive theme. The lights are given a celebrity 'switch on' in November, and they are there to be admired until Twelfth Night. An evening visit to this part of town also permits some vigorous window-shopping at Selfridges and the other stores of Oxford Street, and Hamleys and Liberty on Regent Street. Fortnum & Mason on Piccadilly usually puts on a good display as well (and its windows are worth a special look at any time of year). Do note that, in the run-up to Christmas, the whole of the West End can be surprisingly crowded well after the shops have closed. / Tube: Marble Arch, Oxford Circus, Bond Street, Piccadilly Circus.

Christmas Tree WC2
Trafalgar Sq
The great Christmas Tree in Trafalgar Square, decorated with its bright white lamps, is an annual gift from the people of Oslo to the people of London. There are regular carol concerts around the tree. / Tube: Charing Cross.

New Year's Eve
Packing yourself into Trafalgar Square WC2 is traditionally the way to see in the New Year in London (although recently the event has been a bit of a damp squib, thanks to the pedestrianisation works in the square and the apparent antipathy Mr Mayor has to anybody celebrating anything in the capital: maybe when the digging has finished the occasion will return to normal.) Those who do not like crowds should definitely stay away, and even those who do should think twice – as midnight approaches the drunken crush can be absolutely unbearable and it can be so crowded as to be impossible to get into the Square itself. Getting home is, unusually, free of charge as London Transport operates its annual (usually sponsored)

offer of free transport throughout the capital, with the tubes running well past midnight. If you'd like to consider an alternative, you could spend the evening spanning two hemispheres – the Greenwich and Docklands Festival (see above for details and website) organise a free New Year's Eve event called First Night, with fireworks and street entertainments, centred on Greenwich town centre.

Spitalfields Winter Festival* E1
Shoreditch Church, Shoreditch High St
Hotline (020) 7377 1362
See the Summer Festival (June) for details. The Winter Festival – apart from the obvious Christmas theme and carol singing – is very similar. / Times: festival, details from hotline or website; www.spitalfieldsfestival.org.uk; Tube: Old Street, Liverpool Street.

Entertainments

Radio & Television

London's position as a great centre of music and broadcasting means that there's a huge amount of entertainment of every kind being produced – from classical concerts to game-shows. And it's there just for the asking, as being a member of the studio audience is invariably free.

Below, we give details of organisations which produce concerts and shows, both for radio and TV. If you really want to see a particular programme (not produced by one of these companies) there's no substitute for tracking down the production company and asking how it allocates tickets.

Radio – BBC W12

Audience Services, PO Box 3000, London W12 7RJ
Recorded information (020) 8576 1227
Radio shows tend to be scheduled only about six weeks ahead, so audience tickets are often available at short notice. You might listen to a recording of The Now Show or Brain of Britain. The recorded information service tells you what's on offer and they will, on request, put your name on a mailing list (but currently, there is only one for radio comedy) and you will be kept up to date with what's available in that type of entertainment. There's something for almost all tastes, from classical concerts, via easy listening, to quiz programmes. Radio shows are mainly recorded at the BBC Radio Theatre at Broadcasting House W1 and concerts are usually at the Maida Vale Studios, Delaware Road W9. / www.bbc.co.uk/tickets.

Television – BBC W12

Audience Services, Room 309, Design Building, Television Centre, London W12 7RJ   (020) 8576 1227
There's a huge choice of comedies, variety shows, quiz programmes and debates you can watch being recorded during the afternoon and evening. Ring to check there is a series coming up and that the BBC makes the programme you want to see (some are filmed by separate production companies – Have I Got News For You is made by Hat Trick Productions, for example, see also) and ask for information about what's currently on offer, or send an SAE to Audience Services. People drop out at short notice so it is worth trying for shows happening in the near future. Singles and parties are welcome, and this is an ideal outing for all ages that costs no more than the coach hire. Children aged under 14 are not generally admitted. Further information is also available via email: tv.ticket.unit@bbc.co.uk. / www.bbc.co.uk.

Television – Channel 5 WC2E
22 Long Acre   (0845) 7050505
Companies making programmes for the newest of England's terrestrial TV stations may advertise for audience members, for example in Time Out. *Channel 5 does not have a mailing list but you can keep up-to-date with what's available via the Duty Office.* / www.channel5.co.uk.

Television – Hat Trick Productions W1
10 Livonia St   (020) 7287 1598
Most famous for Have I Got News for You *and* Who's Line is it Anyway?, *this independent company also made* Drop the Dead Donkey *and* Father Ted. *There's no mailing list and it seems regulars call the ticketline every six weeks or so to check availability (tickets are also available from a website). You stand a fair chance of getting tickets for your favourite show, but only if you start trying several months in advance. Generally, the minimum age for children attending a show is 15. Most recording is at the London Studios on the South Bank.* / www.hattrick.co.uk.

Television – LWT SE1
London Studios, Upper Ground   (020) 7620 1620
This ITV company, which produces shows at its studios on the South Bank, runs a mailing list for people wishing to apply for tickets. Write or telephone to put your name on the list. (The website also lists other ITV companies whose shows may also be filmed in London, such as The Pepsi Chart.) / www.itv.co.uk.

Music

Most of the major arts centres offer free foyer music (often of very high quality) on a regular basis. Details are given under the entries for the respective venues – see the **Royal Festival Hall** and the **Royal National Theatre** (South), the **Royal Opera House** (Central) and the **Barbican** (City). Other places listed which offer regular free music include **Westminster Abbey** (Central), **St Mary Abbots** (West), **Christchurch Spitalfields** (City) and the **Union Chapel** (North).

As a major centre of popular, modern music, the capital boasts a number of world-renowned clubs and music venues. While the majority, unfortunately, charge entrance fees, there are still quite a number of places to hear rock, dance, jazz or world music for free. Major music and book stores – HMV, Virgin Records, Borders and Tower Records – host live performances and album release concerts from time to time.

For free live shows at music venues, Mon or Tue evenings are generally the best bet. In addition, on many nights, free admission can be had by arriving early in the evening, say, before 9pm.

Entertainments

One of the most reliable options for seeing live music is in bars and pubs, which offer intimate settings for performances. A popular pub event is the 'open mic night', in which any sort of aspiring artist, from folk singer to diva, can take the stage. These showcases provide a good opportunity to hear a wide range of musical tastes, and perhaps even see a future star. A number of periodicals, such as *Time Out* (which specifically notes free evenings) list musical happenings. Better yet, check your 'local' for upcoming gigs.

City Music

There is music in one of the many churches of the City almost every lunchtime – almost all concerts begin between 1pm and 1.15pm and generally last no more than an hour. A useful monthly publication, City Events, available from the City of London Information Centre by St Paul's, gives advance details. Alternatively, if you arrive at the centre by 12.40pm you should have time to locate the concert of your choice and walk to the appropriate church.

The top time of year for City music is during the City of London Festival (see also) in late June/early July.

The Corporation of London also presents a series of band concerts through the summer at three locations (Finsbury Circus, Tower Place and Royal Exchange Forecourt) from noon to 2pm (July – Aug) – you can get a leaflet from the Information Centre for dates and times. / Tube: Bank, St Paul's.

Events in the Royal Parks
(020) 7298 2000
Most of the Royal Parks (Hyde, Regent's, St James's, Green, Greenwich and Richmond, and Kensington Gardens) have music, and other events, on a regular basis. It's well worth sending an A5 SAE to Old Police House, Hyde Park, London W2 2UH (tel (020) 7298 2000), asking for a Summer Entertainment Programme, or check the website. Events of interest to adults include theatrical and operatic productions, dancing demonstrations and guided nature and gardening tours of the parks. For children, there are circus acts and puppet shows. / www.royalparks.co.uk.

Guildhall School of Music & Drama* EC2
Barbican, Silk St   (020) 7382 7192   5–1C
Opera, jazz, ensemble, contemporary music... performances, most of which are free, take place at the School, at the Barbican, and elsewhere, lunchtimes and evenings. Call for the termly programme which gives full details. / www.gsmd.ac.uk; Tube: Moorgate, Barbican.

Music colleges

*London boasts some of the finest music colleges in the world
and, to those who enjoy classical music they represent an
extremely fertile source of free entertainment.*

*All the schools listed give three or four concerts or recitals a
week during their term times. The most popular performances
tend to be the larger ones – those with symphony orchestras or
pieces with a large chorus – of which there may be five or so in
a term at any given school.*

Royal Academy of Music NW1

Marylebone Rd   (020) 7873 7300   2–1A
*Details of some ten free events a week are listed in the termly
Diary of Events (available from the box office on the number
given). In general, lunchtime concerts take place Tue-Thu at
1.05pm in the foyer, while early-evening concerts take place on
Tue at 5.05pm in the Duke's Hall. In addition, there are various
other evening concerts, showcasing classical, jazz and chamber
music. Also there is a chamber music series called* Free on
Fridays *which is designed to show off the Academy's best
performers. The concerts begin at 1.05pm and last about an
hour. (See also the York Gate Collections, page 93).*
/ www.ram.ac.uk; Tube: Baker Street; Café.

Royal College of Music SW7

Prince Consort Rd   (020) 7589 3643 ext 4380   3–1B
*Most performances are given at the college, just behind the
Royal Albert Hall, although quite a number are held at other
venues around the capital. For example, at 1.05pm on Fridays
during term time, a concert is given at the imposing Church of
St Mary Abbots in the centre of Kensington (tube: High Street
Kensington). Lunchtime concerts (Mon-Thu, beginning at
1.05pm) take place variously in the Recital Hall, the Concert
Hall and St Mary Abbots, so check the website or ring for
details. / www.rcm.ac.uk; Tube: (College) South Kensington.*

Royal Opera House* WC2

Covent Garden   (020) 7304 4000 (Box office)   2–2D
*A multi-million pound refurbishment has given the Royal Opera
House several new 'spaces', one of which is the Linbury Studio
Theatre, where free chamber music concerts are given on
Mondays at 1pm. Visitors to the Opera House are also able to
see the recently-refurbished foyer areas and view permanent
displays and temporary exhibitions situated around the
building. (Some areas may be unavailable if events are taking
place during the day.)*

*A great opportunity to get a taste of opera or ballet for free is
the BP Opera and Ballet in the Piazza, a rolling programme
featuring three live relays annually – performances happening
within the opera house are broadcast live to the masses seated
in the market square (weather permitting). Check the website
for further details. / Times: Opera House from 10am; Vilar Floral Hall
10am-3.30pm; www.royalopera.org; Tube: Covent Garden.*

Entertainments

Shell LSO Music Scholarship Final

The £6,000 Shell LSO Music Scholarship (established in 1977) is one of the most prestigious prizes available to young musicians. It follows a four-year cycle covering the four sections of the orchestra; woodwind, strings, brass & timpani, and percussion. In 2003 it will be the turn of the brass. The competition final is held in late June/early July each year and involves the LSO performing selected movements with the four competitors. It's a very enjoyable event if you like listening to classical music in a very informal atmosphere. Tickets are allocated on a first-come, first-served basis by the host venue – typically the Royal Festival Hall or Barbican. For more information call the LSO Scholarship Administrator on (01223) 501709 or see the web site.
/ www.lso.co.uk/discovery/scholarship/home.html.

South Bank Centre SE1

Belvedere Rd   (020) 7960 4242   2–3D
Call for details of performances. / Times: 10am-10.30pm; www.rfh.org.uk; Tube: Waterloo or Embankment.

Trinity College of Music SE10

King Charles Court, Old Royal Naval College, Greenwich
(020) 8305 3888   2–1A
In addition to performances, there are occasional musical competitions and large-scale concerts. Most of the concerts and recitals take place around 1pm in the college, as well as the Regency Hall and churches around London. Not all are free so check ahead for details (a Diary of Events can be obtained from the number given). / www.tcm.ac.uk; Tube: Bond Street.

Central London

Introduction

The fact that Central London is at the ceremonial and governmental heart of Britain – comprising as it does the **Houses of Parliament**, **Westminster Abbey**, **Buckingham Palace** and 10 Downing Street – provides an almost unequalled range of famous historic attractions. The Abbey and Parliament can be visited, but only with a degree of planning.

Another major theme is art and antiquities – this area contains some of the most significant museums and art galleries in the world, such as the **British Museum** and the **National Gallery**. There are, however, also smaller attractions with first-rate collections – among these the **Wallace Collection** and **Sir John Soane's Museum** stand out. In addition, the commercial art world provides a huge and ever-changing selection of pictures and objects to view, and the institutions which deal in them have their own special interest and charm. A visit to one of the great auctioneers, **Sotheby's** or **Christie's**, combines art with theatre. (For a guide to the commercial galleries, see Galleries on page 14).

Central London is a window-shopper's paradise, containing as it does most of the UK's top shops – ranging from **Harrods**, **Selfridges** and **Fortnum & Mason** at the larger end of the scale to the opulent boutiques of **Old Bond Street**, and the charming, small shops in the Regency **Burlington Arcade**. Almost all of the very central areas have sufficient character to justify just strolling around, but **Covent Garden** should be on most lists, as it boasts outdoor entertainers and a variety of festivals year-round.

With children, this can be a rather tiring area. There are the sights of course – **Trafalgar Square**, recently refurbished, and **Eros** can be added to those already mentioned – and there is also the possibility of a trip to **Hamleys**, the world-famous toy shop. Leaving this aside, the top attractions for families are probably **St James's Park** – which is pretty and interesting enough to provide something for everyone – and **Coram's Fields**, a useful amenity for kids in Bloomsbury.

London Tourist Board SW1
Victoria St   2–4B
The main outlet of London's tourist board is within Victoria Station. (See entry on page 11) / www.londontown.com; Tube: Victoria.

Suggested walks

To orientate yourself within central London, try one of these three interesting walks below – one 'historical', one 'intellectual' and the third 'cultural'.

"Historical"

The first stroll encompasses London's most impressive historical sights. Begin at Trafalgar Square, making sure to dodge the buses and pigeons (not always in that order). To the west stretches Pall Mall. Stroll down this wide avenue, flanked by impressive gentlemen's clubs, until reaching St James's Palace. (If you get there by 11.15am, you can follow the St James's Palace detachment of the Queen's Guard as it marches to Buckingham Palace – this walk is not short of picture opportunities, as the throngs of tourists will attest.) From Buckingham Palace, one is a short distance from the immaculate St. James's Park – one of the oldest royal parks. Enter on the western edge of the park, walking alongside the lake and passing Duck Island. Exit at the southeast corner and follow Great George Street towards Westminster. The Abbey and the Houses of Parliament will soon come into view. From this point, the final stage of the walk begins. Head north along Parliament Street, which becomes Whitehall, past Downing Street, the Horse Guards and finally back to Trafalgar Square.

"Intellectual"

Our second recommended walk also begins at Trafalgar Square, but heads north, rather than west. Begin by walking up Charing Cross Road. As you pass Leicester Square to your left, and Long Acre to your right, a long literary path unfolds – a book-lover's dream. Along each side of Charing Cross Road until Oxford Street lies almost the full gamut of booksellers – from the niche specialists to the commercial giants – making for an interesting afternoon within the heart of town.

"Cultural"

For a less intellectually strenuous jaunt, begin at Leicester Square and head north along Leicester Place to Lisle Street. Immediately, the colourful restaurants, markets and stores of Chinatown are in full view. Move west to Wardour Street and turn right. Gerrard Street on the right is the pedestrianised centre of Chinatown. Head further north up Wardour Street and you will be thrust into the crowded, teeming streets of Soho. Slowly the area becomes a mix of the chic, the colourful and the exotic. Soho and its environs has something for all tastes, from galleries and gay bars to 'adult' entertainment options and a variety of restaurants. You can move easily in any direction off Wardour Street to explore the secrets of Soho. Perhaps turn left on to Broadwick Street which will lead you to Carnaby Street – the home of swinging '60s London, re-inventing itself once more as a fashion hot-spot after years of being populated with tourist-trap shops. Inevitably, your wanderings will take you to one of the boundaries of Soho – Oxford Street to the north, Regent Street to the west and Charing Cross Road to the east. On all three streets, there are tube stations and bus stops, making a nice end point for your journey.

Indoor attractions

Alfred Dunhill SW1
48 Jermyn St   (020) 7290 8622   2–3B
Jermyn Street, London's most discreet shopping thoroughfare, boasts the headquarters of one of the more successful brand names in the international luxury branded goods market. The Alfred Dunhill Museum houses examples of motoring accessories, jewellery, watches, handbags and smoking items manufactured by the company over the last century. Give a weeks notice and you can arrange a guided tour (phone for details). / Times: Mon-Sat 9.30am (Sat 10am)-6pm; www.dunhill.com; Tube: Green Park, Piccadilly Circus.

Architectural Association WC1
34-36 Bedford Sq   (020) 7887 4000,
recorded information (020) 7887 4111   2–1C
For anyone with an interest in architecture, the Association offers a rich and varied programme of afternoon and evening lectures. There are also project exhibitions by contemporary architects and students in the Exhibition Gallery and Photo Library throughout the year. Call to find out times of lectures. / Times: Mon-Sat 10am-7pm (Sat 3pm); www.aaschool.ac.uk; Tube: Tottenham Court Road; Café, Restaurant, Picnic area (12pm-2pm).

Architecture Foundation EC1
(020) 7253 3334   2–3B
This body is "dedicated to the display and discussion of contemporary architecture and the built environment in a way that appeals to the public". In addition to an exhibition programme, it holds a series of forums on architectural and urban planning questions, to which the public is invited. Exhibitions are held 2-6 times a year in a variety of different locations in London (as they no longer have a permanent site) – call or check the website for details / Times: telephone only; mon-fri;9.30am-6.00pm; www.architecturefoundation.org.uk.

Ben Uri Art Society NW8
108 Boundary Rd   (020) 7604 3991   4–3A
*The collection includes more than 1000 works by Jewish artists
including Bomberg, Auerbach, Epstein and Kitaj. For further
information of when and what, please check
the website. There are always temporary exhibitions, some of
which are free (phone for details).* / Times: some exhibitions are free;
www.benuri.com; Tube: Swiss Cottage.

BOC Museum WC1
Association of Anaesthetists of GB & Ireland,
21 Portland Pl   (020) 7631 1650   2–1C
*The museum is home to one of the largest collections of early
and contemporary anaesthetic equipment in the world. Each
year a special topic is presented, illustrated with a selection
from the 5,000 items in the collection.* / Times: by telephone
appointment with the Archivist; www.aagbi.org; Tube: Oxford Circus; Café,
Restaurant.

Bonhams SW7
Montpelier St   (020) 7393 3900   3–1C
*If you're in the market for a fine and rare cased self opening
20-bore Royal Brevis side-lock ejector sporting gun by Holland
& Holland or a brilliant-cut diamond heart-shaped pendant
or, as a reader of this book just want a look at such items –
Bonhams art auctions may be the place for you.* / Times: Mon-Fri
9am- 5: 00pm, (switchboard open until 5.30pm) Sun 11am-3pm;
www.bonhams.com; Tube: Swiss Cottage.

Borders WC2
120 Charing Cross Rd   (020) 7379 8877   2–2C
*Many bookshops do author signings nowadays, but it was this
huge American book chain which really pioneered in-store
entertainment, and it continues to pursue an active diary of
events. Along with a comprehensive programme of book
signings, there are also quiz nights, discussion groups, poetry
readings (and 'open mic sessions') and children storytimes.
Ring the store, or check the website or Metro for details –
there is also a branch at 203 Oxford Street (tel 7292 1600).*
/ Times: Mon-Sat 9am-11pm, Sun 12pm-6pm; www.bordersstores.co.uk;
Tube: Tottenham Court Road; Café.

British Museum WC1
Great Russell St   (020) 7323 8000   2–1C
Six million visitors a year can't be wrong – this august neo-classical building (Robert Smirke, 1823-52) is London's leading attraction – free or otherwise. It does, after all, house what is arguably the world's greatest collection of antiquities. The museum has been undergoing a series of renovations and redevelopments, in preparation for its 250th anniversary in 2003. The greatest of these is the Great Court, which has transformed the previously-hidden inner courtyard into one of London's greatest public spaces. The two-acre square, with the great Round Reading Room at its centre, has been enclosed by a spectacular glass roof.

Particular strengths of the collection include Egyptian antiquities, coins and medals, the collections relating to Greek and Roman civilisation (especially, of course, the marbles from the Parthenon), clocks, and prints and drawings. No-one could possibly take in the whole museum in a day – just to pass by all the exhibits would apparently require a walk of some two and a half miles – so it's probably worth deciding on a section of particular interest and trying to make sense of that. From Mon-Fri, the museum's experts give gallery talks at 11.15am and lectures at 1.15pm. Free daily 'eyeOpener' tours, which focus on different areas of the museum, run all day and last approximately 50 minutes. There are many interesting temporary exhibitions (mostly free of charge) and there are regular talks and films, and even occasional art workshops for children. / Times: Sun-Wed 10am-5.30pm, Thur-Fri 10am-8.30pm (selected galleries only); www.thebritishmuseum.ac.uk; Tube: Russell Square, Tottenham Court Road, Holborn; Café, Restaurant.

Burlington Arcade W1
Piccadilly   2–2B
This Regency shopping arcade is perhaps the most timeless place in London for window-shopping. Top-hatted beadles maintain standards – no running, no singing, no carrying large parcels, etc – leaving you in perfect serenity to survey the displays in the windows of the small, elegant shops, some of which still sell hand-made luxury goods. / Times: Mon-Sat 9am-6pm; www.burlington-arcade.co.uk; Tube: Green Park, Piccadilly Circus.

Canada House SW1
Trafalgar Sq (entrance on Cockspur St)   (020) 7258 6600
2–2C
Overlooking Trafalgar Square, the home of the Canadian High Commission (restored in 1998) was built by Sir Robert Smirke, who also designed the British Museum. There are regular themed exhibitions, at which visitors can obtain information about everything Canadian, from the arts to history. There is free internet service for those wishing to use the computers to do any kind of research on Canada and – for Canadians only – to check e-mail. / Times: Mon-Fri 10am-6pm; www.dfait-maeci.gc.ca/london; Tube: Charing Cross.

Cartoon Art Trust WC1

7 Brunswick Centre, Bernard St   (020) 7278 7172   2–1D
The Cartoon Art Trust (formerly the National Museum of Cartoon Art) displays all forms of cartoon art, from stick figures to 3-dimensional drawings, with various exhibitions and displays during the year in its two galleries. A recent exhibition, Kings and Queens, focused on representations of the monarchy throughout history. Entrance is free, but donations are appreciated. / Times: Mon-Fri 12pm-8pm; www.cartoonarttrust.co.uk; Tube: Russell Square; Café, Restaurant, Picnic area.

Christie's SW1 6QT

8 King St   (020) 7839 9060   2–3B
The two great international auction-houses (the other, of course, is Sotheby's, which has its own entry, see also) both originated in London. Christie's has been helping collectors build up, and in later generations dispose of, great collections of pictures and furniture since 1766. Except for the grandest of sales (to which admission is restricted to those who have bought catalogues), you are welcome to have a look at the goods to be auctioned in the days before the sale and, indeed, to attend the auction itself – one of the best free shows in town. / Times: Mon-Fri 9. 00am-4.30pm (Tue 8pm), Sun 2pm-4.30pm(gen); www.christies.com; Tube: Green Park.

City Yeomanry Museum WC2

10 Stone Buildings, Lincolns Inn   (020) 8506 1888   5–2A
A small museum whose permanent exhibit includes uniforms, medals and equipment of the Inns of Court Regiment and the City of London Yeomanry dating from the Napoleonic Wars. / Times: by appt only Mon-Fri 10am-4pm; www.army.mod.uk/ceremonialandheritage/museums/details/m107inns.htm; Tube: Chancery Lane.

Contemporary Applied Art W1

2 Percy St   (020) 7436 2344   2–1C
At Britain's largest gallery specialising in the exhibition and sale of contemporary crafts you find jewellery, fine metalwork, ceramics, wood, textiles, furniture, glass and paper. Seven exhibitions are held a year – they are free to attend but, as everything is for sale, your visit could turn out to be expensive! / Times: Mon-Sat 10.30am-5.30pm; www.caa.org.uk; Tube: Goodge Street, Tottenham Court Road.

Central London

Courtauld Gallery* WC2
Somerset House, Strand   (020) 7848 2777,
recorded information (020) 7848 2526   2–2D
*This world-renowned gallery features a rich collection of works
– from the Renaissance to the 20th Century. Included
in the collection is Manet's Bar at the Folies-Bergères and
Van Gogh's Self-Portrait with Bandaged Ear. The gallery
benefits from its link to the Courtauld Institute of Art which
holds an art history lecture series on Tuesday evenings. Ring
(020) 7848 2777 for further information. A visit to the gallery
makes a relaxing stop after lunch in nearby Victoria
Embankment Gardens. (See also Somerset House and Gilbert
Collection.)* / Times: Mon 10am-2pm (at all times for under 18's, full time
u.k. students and unemployed); www.courtauld.ac.uk; Tube: Temple, Covent
Garden, Holborn; Café.

Dickens & Jones Personal Beauty Studio W1
224-244 Regent St   (020) 7287 4947   2–2B
*A visit to this team of independent make-up and skin care
artists, headed up by Paul Herrington (celebrity make-up artist
and former lead make-up artist of Space NK) will result in an
individual beauty profile. You can revel in the attention as the
team works to find the best make-up look for you that works
with your skin. Appointments can last up to 90 minutes.*
/ Times: by appt only Mon-Sat 10.15am-4.30pm (Thu 5.30pm); Tube: Oxford
Circus.

Fortnum & Mason W1
181 Piccadilly   (020) 7734 8040   2–2B
*The royal grocers (established on this site in 1707) have all the
accoutrements you could possibly desire of such an
establishment – plush red carpets, glittering chandeliers and
assistants in tailcoats. The shop has particularly impressive
displays of its famous produce, both in the grand ground floor
sales area, expanded in 1998, and in the Piccadilly windows.
The external clock is a well-known landmark – see the outdoor
section.* / Times: Mon-Sat 10am-6.30pm (closed bank holidays);
www.fortnumandmason.com; Tube: Green Park, Piccadilly Circus.

Foyle's WC2
113-119 Charing Cross Rd   (020) 7437 5660   2–2C
*You can potter happily for hours in this establishment –
Britain's largest bookshop in terms of number of titles – which
supposedly carries a copy of almost every book in print,
however esoteric. After many years in decline, there is every
sign that this may once again become one of London's best
bookshops as well as one of the biggest. There is also an art
gallery on the second floor, with free changing exhibitions of
contemporary work.* / Times: Mon-Sat 9.30 am-8. 00pm, Sun 12pm-6pm;
www.foyles.co.uk; Tube: Tottenham Court Road.

Gilbert Collection* WC2

Somerset House, Strand   (020) 7420 9400   2–2D

Sir Arthur Gilbert, a Briton who made his fortune in the US, has chosen the old country as the recipient of his intriguing collection, whose highlights include gold snuff boxes and Italian mosaics. The display, in impressive former cellars of Somerset House, also includes furniture, silver, clocks and portrait miniatures. (See also Somerset House and Courtauld Gallery.)
/ Times: Daily after 4.30pm except during special exhibitions; www.gilbert-collection.org.uk; Tube: Temple; Café, Restaurant.

Grant Museum of Zoology & Comparative Anatomy WC1

Biology Department (Darwin Building), University College, Gower St   (020) 7679 2647   2–1C

This natural history museum holds some 35,000 specimens which range right across the animal kingdom, from an aardvark and gorillas to sloths and a quagga (an extinct type of zebra) – there are skeletons, specimens in jars and real stuffed animals. Although it is primarily a resource for education, the museum is open to anyone by appointment and is popular with photographers and artists. School groups are also welcome.
/ Times: Wed & Fri 1pm-5pm & by appointment: call Helen Chatterjee (e-mail zoology.museum@ucl.ac.uk); //collections.ucl.ac.uk/zoology/default.asp; Tube: Euston, Euston Square, Warren Street or Goodge Street.

Grays Antique Market W1

58 Davies St   (020) 7629 7034   2–2B

There are few destinations in London which offer rare gems and minerals, antique rifles, Islamic Art and the River Tyburn flowing through the basement! These two grand Edwardian buildings, off Bond Street, are home to an antiques market with over 200 stalls and shops (including a large antiquarian book dealer), offering the usual assortment of the useful and useless. However, the true speciality of the place are the regular themed exhibitions – subjects vary widely, from Beatles memorabilia to extensive and ever-popular erotica collections.
/ Times: Mon-Fri 10am-6pm (Sat, Dec only 11am-5pm); www.egrays.co.uk; Tube: Bond Street.

Great Ormond Street Hospital for Children WC1

Peter Pan Gallery, 55 Great Ormond St   (020) 7405 9200   2–1D

An exhibition relating to the history of this famous children's hospital, founded in 1852, is housed in a neighbouring Georgian town house. Exhibits include photographs and ephemera. Since 1929 the hospital has received the copyright proceeds from sales of J M Barrie's Peter Pan (extended in perpetuity in the UK by a unique Act of Parliament in 1987 when the copyright expired), and there are letters from the author as well as copies of the book in a number of languages (unfortunately the letters are not on display and can only be viewed by prior request). / Times: by appointment, Mon-Fri 9.30am-4.30pm; www.gosh.org; Tube: Russell Square, Holborn, Euston.

Hamleys W1
188 -196 Regent St   (020) 7494 2000   2–2B

At Christmas it's unbearably crowded, but all year round, this is the number one destination on any child's tour of London – the world's largest toyshop. Highlights from the seven jam-packed floors include moving displays, talking books, a haunted staircase and a huge model railway. / Times: Mon-fri 10am- 8pm, sat 9.30am-8pm Sun 12pm-6pm; www.hamleys.co.uk; Tube: Piccadilly Circus, Oxford Circus; Café.

Harrods SW1
Knightsbridge   (020) 7730 1234   3–1D

Europe's most famous department store works very hard to ensure there is always something new to see in its 25 acres of sales space. First-time visitors should not miss the Food Halls, with their intriguing décor and amazing arrangements of produce, but it is the sheer scale of the whole building and the opulence of some of the goods which are probably the main attractions. Special exhibitions are sometimes organised in the ground floor Central Hall. Harrods is a little sensitive about its role as a free tourist attraction – security guards may not allow large parties or people with big bags, dress should be appropriate and photography is not allowed. / Times: Mon-Sat 10am-7pm; www.harrods.com; Tube: Knightsbridge.

Harvey Nichols SW1
109-125 Knightsbridge   (020) 7235 5000   3–1D

Harvey Nichols is a smaller, more intimate department store than its better-known Knightsbridge neighbour and not, therefore, quite as suited to sightseeing. The particularly innovative window displays are always interesting, though, and the glamorous foodie complex on the fifth floor is worth a look for the sheer improbability of its Dan Dare-style architecture and location. / Times: Mon, Tue & Sat 10am-7pm (Wed, Thu & Fri 8pm), Sun 12pm-6pm; www.harveynichols.com; Tube: Knightsbridge.

Houses of Parliament SW1
(020) 7219 3000   2–3C
No visitor will wish to miss the sight of the Palace of Westminster, with its famous clock tower (whose bell is known as Big Ben). There has been a royal palace here since the 11th century, but after a disastrous fire in 1835, the building was reconstructed in neo-Gothic style to the designs of Charles Barry and Augustus Pugin.

The building is not generally open to the public, but if you want to see the fine interior – or our ancient democracy at work – there are two ways of going about it. One is to arrange to go on a tour and the other is to watch a debate – in the Commons or Lords (from one of the Strangers' Galleries) or in a Commons committee. Dealing with the former first, UK citizens wishing to have a tour must apply to their MP in writing, and should do so well in advance. Owing to the recent changes in the sitting hours of both Houses, it is no longer possible to provide overseas visitors with permits to tour the Houses of Parliament during session. However, they can visit during summer opening – check website for details. Tours of the Palace include the 14th century Westminster Hall, where Charles I was tried in 1649. (Tours are usually only available Mon-Wed mornings & Fri afternoons; this varies during parliamentary recesses.)

If you want to watch a debate in progress, the galleries are open to the public. However, priority is given to those with tickets, and the safest course, therefore, to avoid a lengthy queue, is to apply for a ticket, as far in advance as possible, to your MP (or, if you are not a UK citizen, to your embassy or High Commission). Impromptu visitors have a good chance of gaining admission (unless the subject of debate is very controversial) later on in the day – sittings usually go on until 10pm, and sometimes beyond – or on Fri.

If you're planning any visit to Parliament, it's a very good idea to check out your plans with the Public Information Office on the number given. / www.parliament.uk; Tube: Westminster.

Liberty W1
214-220 Regent St   (020) 7734 1234   2–2B
Liberty is one of the most charming and individualistic of London's department stores. It occupies very characterful mock-Tudor premises (built in the '20s, from timbers of two men o'war, HMS Impregnable and HMS Hindustan), which are certainly worth a look, especially the creaky staircases. The store's particular strength is house furnishings and it carries many interesting and unusual objects and fabrics, as well as fashions and cosmetics. / Times: Mon-Wed 10am-6.30pm (Thu 8pm, Fri & Sat 7pm), Sun 12pm-6pm; www.liberty.co.uk; Tube: Oxford Circus; Café, Restaurant.

The Library & Museum of Freemasonry WC2
Great Queen St   (020) 7395 9258   2–2D
If you have always been fascinated by the aura of secrecy of Freemasonry, it may come as a surprise that the Masons are very pleased for you to visit their daunting Grand Temple in Covent Garden. The current monolith was dedicated in 1933, but the site has been associated with Freemasonry for over two centuries. The Library and Museum (with collections of porcelain, glassware, jewels, regalia and Masonic memorabilia) are open to the public. For information about tours of the building, call 7395 9257. / Times: Mon-Fri 10am-5pm, Sat by appointment only; www.grandlodge-england.org; Tube: Holborn, Covent Garden.

London Brass Rubbing Centre* WC2
The Crypt, St Martin-in-the-Fields Church
(020) 7930 9306   2–2C
This charming workshop area is just off the crypt café. Visitors can view brass rubbings, many of which feature knights in armour ready for the joust, and watch modern-day enthusiasts taking rubbings. The exhibition is free, but there is a fee to make a rubbing. / Times: 10am (Sun 12pm)-6pm; www.stmartin-in-the-fields.org; Tube: Charing Cross; Café.

London Scottish Regimental Museum SW1
95 Horseferry Rd   (020) 7630 1639   2–4C
The collection covers the Regiment's uniforms and equipment since its formation in 1859. Exhibits include medals (the regiment has three VCs to its credit), the three war memorials in the Drill Hall, badges, an indexed record of previous members as well as hundreds of photos documenting the history of the Regiment. / Times: by telephone appointment Mon-Fri 9am-4pm; www.londonscottish regt.org.uk; Tube: St James's Park.

National Gallery WC2

Trafalgar Sq   (020) 7747 2885   2–2C

One of the world's great galleries of Western European paintings (some 2300 in number), from the late c13 to the early c20 – Giotto to Picasso. What distinguishes it is the balance of its collection across all of the schools, with practically no great master unrepresented. The Sainsbury Wing (1991) houses the earliest works from 1260 to 1510 (including Botticelli, Bellini and Raphael), and the rest of the collection progresses chronologically through the West Wing (Michelangelo, Holbein, Titian), the North Wing (Rubens, Velázquez, Rembrandt) and the East Wing (Gainsborough, Turner, Constable, Monet, van Gogh), up to 1900. Daily tours of the collection take place (Mon-Sat), at 11.30am & 2.30pm (also Wed at 6.30pm), according to the season, and there are lectures or films about artists or schools of painting at 1pm (daily, Fri 1.15pm). In addition there are free family talks on Sat at 11.30am and 2.30pm. Every Wed evening, student musicians from the Royal College of Music perform in the Central Hall – for information, pick up a copy of The National Gallery News. *If you prefer to let your fingers do the walking (or have a child, of any age, to amuse), don't miss the Micro Gallery Computer Information Room, a great resource for research. There is a charge for some special exhibitions.*
/ *Times: Mon-Sun 10am-6pm (Wed 9pm); www.nationalgallery.org.uk; Tube: Charing Cross, Leicester Square, Embankment; Café, Restaurant.*

National Portrait Gallery* WC2

St Martin's Place   (020) 7306 0055,
recorded information (020) 7312 2463   2–2C

This is arguably the most accessible of London's major galleries. Though in most collections it's artistic merit which wins a place, here it's the importance of the subject of the portrait as much as the eminence of the painter, sculptor or photographer (though many of the great British artists are, of course, represented). Almost all of the major figures of English history are recorded, with the contemporary portraiture galleries being the most popular. The Ondaatje Wing (opened in May 2000) increased the exhibition space by a half, and includes an IT gallery, lecture theatre, roof-top restaurant (with panoramic city views) and a balcony gallery which specialises in faces from British cultural history. One of the longest escalators in the UK transports visitors up to the top floor, from which they can view the collection chronologically as they return to ground level. On Tue-Thu at 1.10pm (Sat & Sun, 3pm), there is a lecture on some aspect of the collection, and on Fri at 6.30pm, musicians perform in the Ondaatje Wing. There is also a variety of temporary exhibitions, for some of which there is a charge.
/ *Times: Mon-Sun 10am-6pm (Thu & Fri 9pm); www.npg.org.uk; Tube: Leicester Square, Charing Cross; Café, Restaurant.*

Percival David Foundation of Chinese Art WC1
53 Gordon Sq   (020) 7387 3909   2–1C
The finest collection of Chinese ceramics outside China is not nearly as well known as it deserves. There are approximately 1,700 items, reflecting Chinese court taste from the c10 to c18. Particular treasures include a unique pair of blue and white temple vases, whose inscriptions date them to 1351.
/ Times: Mon-Fri 10.30am-5pm; www.soas.ac.uk/PDF/home.html; Tube: Russell Square, Goodge Street, Euston Square.

Petrie Museum of Egyptian Archaeology WC1
University College, Malet Place   (020) 7679 2884   2–1C
An extraordinary collection of Egyptian antiquities, excavated by the eminent archaeologist Sir Flinders Petrie and his followers since 1884. The collection includes about 80,000 objects, but only about 5% are on display. The exhibition is organised to illustrate the development of Egyptian culture from Palaeolithic to Roman and Coptic times. There is also a small Syrian Ptolemaic Roman collection (also excavated by Petrie).
/ Times: Tue-Fri 1pm-5pm, Sat. 10am-1pm; www.petrie.ucl.ac.uk; Tube: Warren Street, Goodge Street, Euston Square, Russel Square; Café, Restaurant.

Phillips W1
101 New Bond St   (020) 7629 6602   2–2B
It may be a little less well known than Sotheby's and Christie's, but this Mayfair auctioneer offers just the same possibilities of getting close to great (and lesser) works of art. (For an introduction to the auction houses, see Christie's.) Items range from furniture to textiles. Access to viewings and sales is free (as are verbal valuations, if you have an item you hope may be of value). / Times: Mon-Fri 8.30am-5pm; www.phillips-auctions.com; Tube: Bond Street.

The Photographers' Gallery WC2
5 & 8 Great Newport St   (020) 7831 1772   2–2C
This large, central space was Britain's first independent gallery devoted to photography. Now over thirty years old, it maintains an ever-changing programme of photographic exhibitions. Details of occasional free tours and forthcoming events are listed in its magazine, GREAT, free in the gallery. The extensive print and book shops are worth a browse, too.
/ Times: Mon-Sun 11am (Sun 12 pm)-6pm; www.photonet.org.uk; Tube: Leicester Square; Café.

Poilâne SW1
46 Elizabeth St   (020) 7808 4910   3–2D
Bread from the great Parisian bakery, Poilâne, has almost mythical status in the foodie world. At great expense, ovens mimicking those in the rue du Cherche-Midi have recently been installed in the heart of Belgravia, and you're welcome to stop by to see them in use. Bread-making tends to have finished by the time they open, but you should catch the croissants – if this weren't a book about doing things for free, we'd suggest you bought one for breakfast! / Times: shop open Mon-Fri 7.30am-7.30pm (Sat 6pm); www.poilane.fr; Tube: Victoria.

RIBA (Royal Institute of British Architects) W1

66 Portland Pl   (020) 7580 5533   2–1B

The Architecture Centre is an international showcase for today and the future, and focuses on awards and competitions. However, it also shows some eccentric exhibitions.
/ Times: Mon-Sat 8am-6pm (Tue 9pm); www.architecture.com; Tube: Great Portland Street, Regents Park; Café.

Royal Academy of Arts* W1

Burlington House, Piccadilly   (020) 7300 8000   2–2B

Although there is a charge for all of the exhibitions (of which the most famous is the annual Summer Exhibition), there is no charge for access to the Academy's charming building. In addition, two of its greatest attractions – one architectural, one artistic – are always on view, gratis. The Sackler Galleries extension, built in 1991, is reckoned by many to be one of the most successful modern additions to any period London building (actual entry to the galleries is not free). The glass-sided lift, designed by Norman Foster, by which the galleries are approached, offers a magical journey from the old to the new, and some of the Academy's sculptures are dramatically displayed outside the galleries. At the far end, in its own white space, is displayed the Academy's greatest artistic treasure, the Michelangelo Tondo – the only example in England of the master's sculpture. There are free tours of the early c18 Private Rooms (usually offered three times a week), which are the most characterful part of the Academy – you need to call in advance for details. / Times: Sun-Thu 10am-6pm; Fri 10am-10pm; www.royalacademy.org.uk; Tube: Piccadilly Circus, Green Park; Café, Restaurant.

Royal College of Physicians NW1

11 St Andrew's Place   (020) 7935 1174   4–4B

This art-based collection includes exhibits dating back to the c16 – including portraits, slides and photographs, busts, medals and miniatures – chronicling famous medical personalities. The works are of particular interest to people researching family history where relatives have been fellows of the College, and the building (Grade I listed) itself attracts students of architecture. / Times: entry by appointment through writing; www.rcplondon.ac.uk; Tube: Regent's Park, Great Portland Street; Café, Restaurant, Picnic area.

Royal Courts of Justice WC2

Strand   (020) 7947 6000   2–2D

Almost all of the most important civil cases in England and Wales end up being tried in this imposing Victorian Gothic building. There are usually at least 50 courts sitting at any one time, so you should be able to find something of interest – trials might cover anything from allocating fault for a serious accident to esoteric 'administrative' law cases, in which people can challenge the Government's exercise of its powers. Children under 16 are not admitted. / Times: Mon-Fri 10am-4pm; Tube: Temple; Café.

St Martin-in-the-Fields WC2
Trafalgar Sq   (020) 7839 8362   2–2C
One of the grandest of London's churches – well, its parish does include Buckingham Palace – and a particularly fine sight when floodlit by night. It was designed by James Gibbs and consecrated in 1726. There are concerts every weekday (except Wed & Thu) at 1.05pm – a perfect break from one of the most hectic parts of London or a suitable finale to a visit to the neighbouring National Gallery (see also). Wed & Sun, there is a choral evensong at 5pm. Check the website for periodic free events, which includes a Harvest Festival attended by the 'Pearly' Kings and Queens (first Sun in October).
/ www.stmartin-in-the-fields.org; Tube: Charing Cross, Embankment; Café.

Selfridges W1
Oxford St   08708 377 377   2–2A
In 1909 Gordon Selfridge wanted to establish a new concept in retailing, by positively encouraging browsing without buying and by getting women to 'have a day out' in Selfridges. This is still true today, with its six floors and over 3000 brands to choose from. Start in the basement and work your way up through household, food, lingerie, health & beauty and fashion. Luckily there are lots of cafés and restaurant in which to rest your weary feet. / Times: Mon-Fri 10am-8pm, Sat 9.30am-8pm, Sun 12pm-6pm; www.selfridges.co.uk; Tube: Bond Street, Marble Arch; Café, Restaurant.

Sir John Soane's Museum* WC2
13 Lincoln's Inn Fields   infoline (020) 7405 2107   2–1D
One of the most extraordinary buildings in the world, this actually consists of three interconnected townhouses. It was built by the great architect between 1792 and 1824, for his own occupation and as a home for his eclectic collection of treasures. The collection includes important (and sometimes fascinating) artefacts from Egyptian, Greek and Roman civilisations. There are also some pictures, most famously Hogarth's series of paintings, The Rake's Progress and The Election. The greatest attraction, however, is just wandering around this labyrinthine house, which you may do without any charge (though you do have to pay for conducted tours and some special exhibitions). 2003 sees a program of restoration and expansion for the museum. The first project involves the restoration of the three courtyards which will enable visitors to eventually walk around them. The second is the slightly more ambitious restoration of No 14 Lincoln's Inn Fields which is to become an Education Centre for Architecture. It will also house the museum's collection of 9000 Robert Adam drawings and 250 historical and architectural models. Both projects are due for completion in 2004. / Times: Tue-Sat 10am-5pm, 1st Tue of month 6pm-9pm; www.soane.org; Tube: Holborn.

Central London

Somerset House WC2
Strand   (020) 7845 4600   2–2D
Somerset House (first built in 1547, and since re-modelled many times) is home to several major art collections (see also Courtauld Institute Gallery and Gilbert Collection). On the lower ground floor visitors may watch a (surprisingly) fascinating video which charts the history and many transformations of the building, from a royal palace washed by the River Thames to the office of public bodies such as the Royal Academy and – more recently – the Inland Revenue. A new exhibition in the King's Barge House tells the story of the old Tudor palace, which once stood on this site, and features objects recovered during the renovation of the Courtyard.

The neo-classical Courtyard (which the building surrounds on all sides) is an impressive open space from which to view the building. The fountains playing there – which springs directly from the granite paving – are London's first major public fountains since Trafalgar Square's were built in 1845. Special choreographed performances occur twice an hour and at night the fountains are lit with fibre-optics to create a dramatic effect. (In the winter months, an ice skating rink sits in the courtyard.) / Times: Mon-Sat 10am-6pm, Sun and bank holiday Mon 12pm-6pm; www.somerset-house.org.uk; Tube: Temple; Café, Restaurant, Picnic area.

Sotheby's W1
34-35 New Bond St   (020) 7293 5000   2–2B
Sotheby's is possibly the best known of the great international art auctioneers. Details of access are broadly as for its competitor, Christie's (see also). / Times: Mon-Fri 9am-4.30pm, occasional weekend viewing; www.sothebys.com; Tube: Bond Street, Green Park; Café.

Tate Britain SW1
Millbank   (020) 7887 8000;
recorded information (020) 7887 8008   2–4C
Tate Britain occupies a particularly charming Westminster building overlooking the Thames. Most British artists of any repute, since 1500, are represented: the Blake and Hogarth collections are particularly fine, and the Clore Galleries house the enormous Turner Bequest. (The Tate's international modern art collection now resides in the Tate Modern, see South.)

The Tate Britain Centenary Development, which opened in 2001, added six new galleries to the building with a new entrance on Atterbury St and co incided with a re-hang of the collection in a new, broadly chronological arrangement.

There are tours of different parts of the collection (lasting about an hour) on weekdays at 11am, 12pm, 1.15pm, 2pm and 3pm, and weekends at 12pm, 2.30pm (Sat only) and 3pm, as well as weekly lectures and films.

The Tate Events leaflet provides detailed information and times or details are available on the website. Almost all of the Tate's attractions are without charge, with the exception of the three large annual shows. / Times: Mon-Sun 10am-5.50pm; www.tate.org.uk; Tube: Pimlico; Café.

Theatre Museum WC2
Russell St   (020) 7943 4700   2–2D
The national theatre museum occupies an appropriately atmospheric West End location just down the street from Covent Garden market. Run by the V&A, it maintains a large collection of materials – costumes, posters, sets, photographs, programmes, props – to illustrate the development of stage performances from Shakespearean times to today. In addition to the displays, they run numerous work-shops and activities – see website for details. / Times: Tue-Sun 10am-6pm, closed 24-26 Dec; theatremuseum.vam.ac.uk; Tube: .

Twinings WC2
216 Strand   (020) 7353 3511   2–2D
Dating from 1706, the shop of the famous tea company claims to be the oldest in London in its original ownership, and selling the same product. It certainly has a lot of period charm and its compact premises (suitable for small parties only) house a collection illustrating the history of Twinings and its involvement in tea. / Times: Mon-Fri 9.30am-4.45pm & the morning of the Lord Mayor's Show, before & after the events; www.twinings.co.uk; Tube: Temple.

University College Art Collection (Flaxman Gallery, The College Art Collections) WC1
Gower St   (020) 7679 7700;
Strang Print Room (020) 7679 2540   2–1C
John Flaxman (1755-1826) was a pre-eminent name in the emergence of neo-classicism in England and in 1810, he became the first Professor of Sculpture at the Royal Academy. Plaster models from which his marble sculptures were subsequently made are on permanent display in the Flaxman Gallery. In the Strang Print Room there is a display which changes each term drawn from the College Art Collections – a diverse assemblage of over 10,000 items dating from 1490 (and including works from Constable, Turner, Durer, Rembrandt and van Dyck as well as early Slade School work from famous artists). / Times: Flaxman Mon-Fri 8.45am-10.30am (Fri 7pm), Sat 9.30am-4.30pm; Strang Print Room Wed-Fri during term time 1pm-5pm; collections.ucl.ac.uk/collart; Tube: Warren Street, Goodge Street.

Wallace Collection W1

Manchester Sq   (020) 7935 0687   2–1A

*Hertford House, an imposing and sumptuous mansion just
north of Oxford Street, contains one of the most splendid
collections of pictures and artefacts in London, bequeathed to
the nation by Lady Wallace in 1897. It has been suggested that
one of the galleries, with its pictures by Watteau and
Fragonard, houses the finest group of French c18 pictures
which can be seen in a single room anywhere. The collection
also includes works by Rembrandt, Rubens and Hals (Laughing
Cavalier). Extraordinary clocks, Sèvres porcelain and armour
are among the other attractions. Free general guided tours are
conducted at 1pm on weekdays (also at 11.30am Wed & Sat
and 3pm Sun).*

*To celebrate the museum's centenary, an extensive project of
renovations was launched. The central courtyard has been
enclosed by an impressive pyramidal glass roof, allowing the re-
instatement of marble sculptures and a bronze fountain placed
there by Sir Richard Wallace. A restaurant, four galleries, a
library and lecture theatre have also been added in recent
times.* / Times: Mon-Sun 10am (Sun 12pm)-5pm; www.the-wallace-
collection.org.uk; Tube: Bond Street; Café, Restaurant.

Westminster Abbey* SW1

(020) 7654 4900   2–3C

*Sadly, in reaction to sheer force of numbers (over 3 million
visitors a year), no part of the interior of this great and historic
church – whose consecration predated the 1066 Invasion – is
now open gratis to the public. You can always attend a service
of course – the choir has a fine reputation – or, if your taste is
for something more secular, there is a short weekly organ
recital at 5.45pm on Sun. Such visits, however, will provide very
limited opportunities to explore the architecture and the many
monuments to famous folk.*

*Admission to the atmospheric cloisters is, however, free. Rebuilt
after a fire in 1298, they would once have been the busiest
parts of the Abbey. One can traverse the cloisters to visit the
College Garden (donations appreciated), where the Abbey's first
Infirmary garden was established in the c11. During July &
August, bands play there on Thu between 12.30pm-2pm.*
/ www.westminster-abbey.org; Tube: Westminster, St James's Park.

Westminster Cathedral* SW1
Victoria St   (020) 7798 9055   2–4C
Completed in 1903, this Byzantine-style Roman Catholic cathedral houses some fine marble work and mosaics, with the sculptures of the 14 Stations of the Cross by Eric Gill being particularly renowned. It is famous for its choir, and services are sung daily except in August. Unfortunately there is a small charge to ascend the campanile (bell tower), which gives a fine view over much of London. Visitors cannot explore the cathedral while services are in progress , but they can look around the bell tower / Times: Mon-Sun 7am (Sat 8am)-7pm; www.westminstercathedral.org.uk; Tube: Victoria.

Westminster City Archives SW1
10 St Ann's St   (020) 7641 5180   2–4C
Most boroughs have an archive, and if you are at all interested in the history of a particular area, make sure to check it out. These can be quite fascinating places, filled with information on all aspects of local life you might never otherwise have considered looking for, and family historians find them a particularly helpful resource. In addition, there are usually exhibitions on aspects of local history. This being Westminster, these particular archives are extensive and are housed in an impressive new building, tucked away behind the Abbey. Over 5 kilometres of shelving hold around 60,000 items – the earliest is dated 1256. / Times: Mon, Fri & Sat 10am-5pm, Tue-Thu 10am-7pm; www.westminster.gov.uk/libraries/index.cfm; Tube: St James's Park.

Outdoor attractions

Berwick Street Market W1
Berwick St   2–2C
It's the characterful, seedy location that is the main attraction of this atmospheric, small street market situated amongst record shops, fabric warehouses and vice dens in Soho. It specialises in cheap fruit and veg and there are also some decent fish, bread and cheese stalls as well as others selling general household goods. / Times: Mon-Sat 9am-5pm; Tube: Piccadilly Circus.

Buckingham Palace* SW1
(020) 7930 4832   2–3B
This house has been the principal residence of the Sovereign only since Victoria's day. You know if Her Majesty is at home because the royal standard (a red, gold and blue quartered flag, with lions and a harp) replaces the Union Flag on the flagpole. The main façade, facing the Mall, is much more recent (1913) than the rest of the building and, as is often noted, gives the impression of nothing so much as a more-important-than-usual branch of Barclays Bank. To get a better (and more sympathetic) feeling of what lies behind the façade, walk down Buckingham Gate, and appreciate the side view of the palace. The Queen's private quarters are on the other side, overlooking Constitution Hill. (There is a charge for the summer tours of the interior of the palace, as there is for admission

to the Queen's Gallery or the Royal Mews.) One of the most opportune times to visit, of course, is for the Changing of the Guard (see also). / www.royal.gov.uk; Tube: St James's Park, Victoria, Green Park.

Charing Cross Collectors Fair WC2
Villiers St   2–2C
A tiny collectors market on the high-level approach to Charing Cross station from Hungerford Bridge, selling stamps, coins and some more touristy items, including football scarves. It's smaller during the week, and less worth a visit. / Times: Sat 8am-5pm; Tube: Charing Cross, Embankment.

Cleopatra's Needle WC2
Victoria Embankment   2–2D
This 3,500-year-old obelisk, weighing about 186 tons, now by the side of the Thames, was taken from near the Temple of the Sun God in Heliopolis in Egypt. It was presented to Britain by the Turkish Viceroy in 1819 and has a twin, which stands in New York's Central Park. The two lions which 'guard' the needle were incorrectly placed (they should actually face away, to keep watch), but their position has never been corrected. / Tube: Embankment.

Coram's Fields* WC1
93 Guilford St   (020) 7837 6138   2–1D
Seven acres of central London to which adults (over 16) are not admitted – unless accompanied by a child! This shady playground – the legacy of an c18 philanthropist – is a boon for harassed parents. It boasts play equipment, a sports area, paddling pool, pets corner and a duck pond. Note: the house in which Charles Dickens lived is quite close, at 48 Doughty Street. / Times: 9am-8pm (Jun-Aug), dusk rest of year; Tube: Russell Square; Café, Restaurant, Picnic area (open School holidays only).

Covent Garden WC2
The Market   (020) 7836 9136   2–2C
Covent Garden, with its c18 market setting and its colourful shops, stalls and cafés, is one of the most agreeable and popular places for a stroll in central London. There's almost invariably something going on in the way of musical performances, busking or more serious street-theatre – the Market office (on the number given) can provide information about forthcoming attractions. Of particular interest is the newly-refurbished Royal Opera House on the east side of Covent Garden. The building's gleaming Floral Hall is now an open public space. (Just north of Covent Garden lies Neal Street. This was formerly a warehouse district, but now is refurbished, with eccentric stores, restaurants and regular street performers.) / www.coventgardenmarket.co.uk; Tube: Covent Garden, Leicester Square; Café.

Central London

Eros SW1
Piccadilly Circus   2–2C
Although invariably known as Eros, the famous, small statue at Piccadilly Circus in fact represents the Angel of Christian Charity. Unveiled in 1893, it was London's first statue to be made of aluminium, at the time a rare and unusual material, and commemorates the philanthropist Lord Shaftesbury (whose Avenue is nearby). / Tube: Piccadilly Circus.

Fortnum & Mason Clock W1
181 Piccadilly   (020) 7734 8040   2–2B
On the hour, every hour, four-foot-high figures of Mr Fortnum and Mr Mason emerge from doors above the shop's main entrance, face each other and bow. A c18 air is then played on 17 bells. The two gentlemen then bow again and retire to their respective quarters. All-in-all, it's quite an amusing performance from one of London's few performing clocks (see also Swiss Centre). / www.fortnumandmason.co .uk; Tube: Piccadilly Circus, Green Park.

Green Park SW1
(020) 7930 1793   2–3B
The park was originally meadowland used for hunting, and duels were regularly fought here until the mid-c17. Now the 53 acres by Piccadilly comprise what the unkind might describe as the Ugly Duckling of the Royal Parks – alone among them, it lacks a lake, flowers, summer music and café. It is, however, a relaxing place and very central. Constitution Hill (which runs along the park's southern border) is so-called in commemoration of Charles II's morning walks. / Times: 24 hours; www.royalparks.gov.uk; Tube: Green Park, Hyde Park Corner; Picnic area.

Old Bond Street W1
2–2B
If you're seriously into window-shopping, you certainly shouldn't miss the extraordinary row of shops to be found in this street which, for more than three centuries, has been one of London's most fashionable boutique thoroughfares – and which is currently enjoying a new wave of popularity. All the shops whose very names conjure up visions of opulence are there – Cartier, Tiffany, Versace, to name but a few. Extravagantly-scaled boutiques of note include Donna Karan, Prada and Ralph Lauren. Most of the best names are in Old Bond Street, but, externally at least, the most impressive shop of all is Asprey (jewellers and goldsmiths) of 165 New Bond Street (under refurbishment at the time of going to press). / Tube: Green Park.

Riverside Walk
See the introduction of the South section for suggestions of interesting walks by the Thames.

Roman Bath* WC2
5 Strand Ln   (020) 7641 5264   2–2D
A whodunnit (or rather 'who built it') mystery surrounds the remains of a bath restored in the c17 and believed by some people to be Roman. It's owned by the National Trust

and there is an entry fee, but if you find your way down the steps and into the narrow lane off the Strand, 90 per cent of what there is to see is visible through the window. Peer in, read the printed notice and decide the origins for yourself. / Times: 24 hours (light switch operational from outside); www.nationaltrust.org.uk; Tube: Temple (not Sun), Blackfriars, Charing Cross.

Speakers' Corner W2
Hyde Park (NE corner)   2–2A
For more than a century, this has been the London home of the soapbox orator – Sunday sees the expression of a kaleidoscope of views, from the slightly off-beat to the decidedly cranky. The 'official' website given lists famous people who have voiced their opinions in the past, and demonstrations which have begun here (including meetings of the Suffragette movement). / Times: Sun afternoon; www.speakerscorner.net; Tube: Marble Arch.

St James's Park SW1
(020) 7930 1793   2–3C
This is possibly the most beautiful, and certainly the most highly cultivated, of the Royal Parks. Situated as it is, in the ceremonial heart of London, between Westminster and Buckingham Palace, it offers idyllic views in both directions. The park (93 acres in extent) was acquired by Henry VIII as a deer park for St James's Palace, but owes much of its current appearance to John Nash, whose designs were commissioned in the reign of George IV. During the summer, there are frequent weekend concerts at the bandstand and gun salutes (see also) on ceremonial occasions. The pelicans are fed at 3pm every afternoon, by Duck Island. / Times: 24 hours; www.royalparks.gov.uk; Tube: St James's Park; Café.

Swiss Centre Clock W1
Leicester Sq   2–2C
The Swiss Centre boasts a fine 27-bell glockenspiel, which plays Brahms, classical Swiss folk tunes and folk music from around the world. It was built in 1985 and dedicated to the City of Westminster to celebrate its 400th anniversary. Sounding the hour takes about five minutes, during which an Alpine procession of cows, sheep, milkmaids, etc makes its way around the base of the clock. There are performances at noon, 6pm, 7pm and 8pm every day, and, at weekends and bank holidays, on the hour every hour, between noon and 8pm, except 1pm. / Times: daily; Tube: Piccadilly Circus, Leicester Square.

Trafalgar Square WC2
2–2C
This great, central square, dominated by the National Gallery (see also) is famous for its 170-foot high column dedicated to the memory of Lord Nelson (1843), its fountains and its pigeons. A major improvement of the area designed to bring out its potential as a 'world space' is drawing to a close as we go to press (pedestrianising its northern edge, and ultimately aiming to make it easier for walkers to progress through it en route to the south bank via Northumberland Avenue). If all goes to plan, the square will become a gathering point for

Londoners – not just a rendezvous for tourists. The statues of imperial lions (Landseer, 1867) remain one of its most prominent features, despite the fact that real lions never sit as represented – they always lie on their side. / Tube: Leicester Square, Charing Cross.

Victoria Embankment Gardens WC2
Villiers St   Festival details:
Alternative Arts (020) 7375 0441   2–2D
This colourful, elongated park lies a few short steps from the traffic and bustle of the Strand. Spring and summer usher in not only a profusion of blooms but also an array of entertainments, such as dance, mime, music, poetry and opera festivals. In spite of its attraction and especially considering the major road running alongside, it is surprisingly peaceful. An ideal spot to lunch – nearby Villiers Street has a plethora of sandwich shops – it's very popular with local office workers. York Watergate (1626) is an attractive curiosity, and there are many plaques and explanatory notices about the history of the area to educate you. The largest of these reminds you that, until the construction of the Embankment in 1828, all of what is today a garden was submerged beneath the Thames!
/ Tube: Charing Cross, Embankment; Café.

Victoria Tower Gardens SW1
Millbank   2–4D
This quiet and extremely scenic garden, beneath the looming presence of the Victoria Tower (at the other end of the Houses of Parliament from Big Ben) is graced by a cast of Rodin's Six Burghers of Calais and a bronze of the Suffragette, Emmeline Pankhurst, More practically, there is also a children's play area.
/ Times: 7am-dusk; Tube: Westminster.

Wellington Arch* W1
Hyde Park Corner   (020) 7930 2726   2–3A
The Wellington Arch bears the largest piece of sculpture in London, Quadriga, by Adrian Jones (1912), in which a figure of Peace descends upon the Chariot of War. The neo-classical Arch itself was built to celebrate the Duke of Wellington's victories over Napoleon, and was completed in 1828, originally bearing a gigantic statue of the Iron Duke himself. Before restoration by English Heritage in 1999, the arch contained London's smallest police station. Colourful new illuminations make night-time visits the most rewarding, and a museum has been opened, for which there is a charge. / Times: Museum 10am-6pm, Wed-Sun (10am-4pm in winter); www.english-heritage.org.uk; Tube: Hyde Park Corner.

West London

Introduction

West London offers a lot of possibilities to those who want to combine a little artistic or intellectual interest (perhaps a trip to the **Victoria & Albert Museum** or the **Serpentine Gallery**) with a visit to one of the beautiful parks which dot the area, such as **Hyde Park**, **Kensington Gardens** or **Holland Park**.

This combination makes it an excellent area for days out with children, for whom the **Natural History Museum** and **Science Museum** are top attractions.

Away from the centre and its famous parks, the area is rich with fine houses and gardens, such as **Osterley Park** and **Chiswick House**. Take a picnic, and both places should, if the weather is fine, provide a good day out. Both houses are convenient for a riverside walk, either for a stroll after lunch or for some more serious exercise. For those who prefer to amble in a more urban environment, the pleasures of Saturday's **Portobello Road market** are hard to beat.

Some lesser-known central attractions well worth investigating include the **Royal Hospital** (and the neighbouring **Ranelagh Gardens**) in Chelsea and **Leighton House Museum and Art Gallery** in Holland Park. Further out, **Pitshanger Manor Museum** and **Gunnersbury Park Museum** offer interesting and attractive houses to visit, set in pleasant parks.

Chelsea Information Office SW3
Old Town Hall, King's Rd   (020) 7352 6056   3–3C
Chelsea's information office is in the same building as a good reference library (the hours are the same for both). Its purpose is to provide information to residents on local council services, but it also tends to attract posters and piles of brochures from organisers of local cultural events. / Times: Mon-Sat 10am-8pm (Wed 1pm, Fri & Sat 5pm); www.rbkc.gov.uk; Tube: Sloane Square, South Kensington.

Hillingdon Tourist Information Centre, Middx
Uxbridge Central Library, High St, Uxbridge
(01895) 250706
The TIC and library keep the same hours. / Times: Mon, Tue & Thu 9.30am-8pm, Wed & Fri 9.30am-5.30pm, Sat 9.30-4pm); www.hillingdon.gov.uk; Tube: Uxbridge.

Hounslow Tourist Information Centre, Middx
Treaty Centre, High St, Hounslow   (020) 8583 2929
The TIC has information on a variety of events including the local May Day festival and the Chiswick Extravaganza at Chiswick House, usually occurring on the August bank holiday weekend. / Times: Mon-Sat 9.30am-5.30pm (Tue & Thu 8pm); www.cip.org.uk; Tube: Hounslow Central.

Twickenham Tourist Information Centre, Middx
Civic Centre, 44 York St   (020) 8891 7272
/ *Times: Mon-Thu 9am-5.15pm (5pm Fri); www.richmond.gov.uk;*
BR: Twickenham.

Suggested walk

A casual walk in this section of London can lead you
through elegant shopping and some charming residential
streets. Begin at Sloane Square and head north along
Sloane Street with its ever more impressive selection of
'designer' stores. Turn left up Pont Street to Beauchamp
Place, famous for its chi-chi shops and 'village'
atmosphere. Keep going and you're on Brompton Road –
turn right and quickly the massive shopping icon of
Harrods looms.

Continue east along the Brompton Road, perhaps,
stopping to admire the designer collections at Harvey
Nichols and its impressive top-floor food hall. At the end
of Brompton Road, cross Knightsbridge to enter Hyde
Park – an ideal spot for a picnic. In the park, stroll along
the Serpentine, perhaps, checking out the latest
contemporary art show at the Serpentine Gallery.

Indoor attractions

Baden-Powell House SW7
65-67 Queen's Gate   (020) 7584 7031   3–2B
*After the death of Baden-Powell in 1941, Boy Scouts around
the world raised money for a 'living memorial'. The result was
this hostel, opened, in 1961. There is a small display about the
life of Baden-Powell and the Scout Movement in the reception
area. (The archives of the movement – dating back to 1907 –
have been moved to a location in Essex; call (020) 8433 7100
for an appointment to view them.)* / *Times: 24 hours;*
www.scoutbase.org.uk; Tube: South Kensington, Gloucester Road; Café.

Boston Manor House, Middx
Boston Manor Rd, Brentford   (020) 8560 5441,
(0845) 456 2800
*Closed for essential works in 2003, but expected to re-open in
2004 – this Jacobean manor was built in 1623 and extended
in 1670, when it was bought by the Clitherow family, whose
home it remained until 1924. The first floor State Rooms have
English Renaissance plaster ceilings and impressive historic
furniture. The drawing room ceiling of 1623 has panels
representing the five senses, the four elements, War & Peace,
Peace & Plenty, and Faith, Hope & Charity. The early c19
ground floor rooms house paintings relating to the locality.*
/ *Times: Sat, Sun & bank hols 2.30pm-5pm, from 1st Sat in Apr to last Sun in
Oct; www.cip.org.uk; Tube: Boston Manor.*

West London

Brompton Oratory SW7
Thurloe Place, Brompton Rd   (020) 7808 0900   3–2C
Popularly but incorrectly known as the 'Brompton Oratory' (real name: Church of the Immaculate Heart of Mary), this imposing South Kensington landmark is the second largest Catholic church in London, with a nave exceeding in width even that of St Paul's Cathedral. Built in a neo-baroque style, it was constructed between 1880-1884 by Cardinal Newman – one of the great religious figures and thinkers of the 19th century. Its choir has something of a reputation and there are three choral services a week as well as during holy festivals. Mass is still said in Latin on Sundays and during Easter.
/ Times: 6.30am-8pm daily; www.brompton-oratory.org.uk; Tube: .

Czech Memorial Scrolls Centre SW7
Kent House, Rutland Gdns   (020) 7581 3741   3–1C
In 1963, 1564 Torah scrolls were acquired from communist Prague – part of the vast collection of Jewish ritual items confiscated by Hitler, who planned to exhibit them in a 'museum of an extinct race'. This exhibition tells their story, something of the history of the communities they came from and of the retrieval of the scrolls by the trust and their subsequent restoration and dispersal to Jewish communities around the world. Beautifully decorated bibles and wimpels are also on display. / Times: Tue & Thu 10am-4pm (other times by appt only); www.czechtorah.org/trust.htm; Tube: Knightsbridge.

Getty Images Gallery SW3
3 Jubilee Place   (020) 7376 4525   3–3C
The Chelsea gallery of a major photo-library, exhibiting a changing selection of prints. / Times: Tue-Fri 10am-6pm, Sat 12pm-6pm; www.hultonarchive.com; Tube: Sloane Square; Café, Restaurant.

Goethe Institut SW7
50 Princes Gate, Exhibition Rd   (020) 7596 4000   3–1C
The Institute, the German cultural centre, has a small gallery which has changing exhibitions of works in some way connected with the country. Small parties (one or two people) can pre-book to view a video from the extensive collection, which includes documentaries and dramas. In early 2001, the gallery re-opened after an extensive refurbishment. The Institute's task is "to promote the German language and to foster international cultural co-operation", to which end it organises various events relating to German culture.
/ Times: Mon-Thu 12pm-8pm, Sat 11am-5pm.; www.goethe.de/london; Tube: South Kensington; Café, Restaurant.

Gunnersbury Park Museum W3
Gunnersbury Park, Popes Ln   (020) 8992 1612   1–3A
This very grand local museum recently celebrated 75 years of opening to the public. It houses a large collection on the history of Ealing and Hounslow, but also temporary exhibitions on wider themes – not always of purely local interest – and there are occasional talks relating to the collections. Housed in a former Rothschild family house, built in 1835 on the site of a former royal residence, it benefits from an extremely pleasant park location. On summer weekends you can visit the original Victorian kitchens. / Times: Apr-Oct 1pm-5pm (Sat, Sun & bank hols 6pm), Nov-Mar 1pm-4pm; kitchens (summer only) 1pm-4pm; www.cip.org.uk/parks/gp/museum.htm; Tube: Acton Town; Café (open summer only).

Heathrow Airport, Middx
Newall Rd   Visitors Centre (020) 8745 6655,
Roof Garden recorded information (020) 8745 5259
Heathrow is staggering in the scale of its operations, handling more than 60 million passengers a year (and more international travellers than any other airport in the world). There is a Visitors Centre, which houses a viewing gallery and an exhibition with interactive technology concerning the airport's past, present and future. Worksheets are available for children. There is also a roof garden between Terminals 1 & 2 (9am-dusk daily). From the viewing area in the Queen's Building, you can watch all the comings and goings of the aeroplanes. / Times: 10am-5pm daily; www.baa.com; Tube: Heathrow Terminals.

Hillingdon Local Heritage Service, Middx
Uxbridge Central Library, High St, Uxbridge
(01895) 250702
The borough doesn't have a dedicated museum but makes do with a small display space in the Central Library. Here you find changing exhibitions and a local studies room. There are periodic events and free internet access for the public. / Times: main library, Mon-Thu 9.30am-8pm (Wed 5.30pm), Fri 10am-5.30pm, Sat 9.30am-4pm; local studies library Mon 9.30am-8pm, Tue-Thu 1am-5.30pm, Fri 10am-12.30pm & 1.30-5.30, Sat 9.30am-12pm & 1am-4pm; www.hillingdon.gov.uk; Tube: Uxbridge.

Hogarth's House W4
Hogarth Ln, Great West Rd   (020) 8994 6757   1–3A
The Chiswick home of the great English engraver and painter William Hogarth (1697-1764) was restored in 1997 to celebrate the tercentenary of his birth. It contains memorabilia of his life, work and circle. The main attractions, however, are his most famous series of engravings (such as Marriage à la Mode and the Rake's Progress) and the attractive garden, which contains a mulberry tree dating from the painter's time. / Times: Tue-Sun 1pm-5pm (Sat & Sun 6pm), (Nov-Mar 5pm); closed January; Tube: Turnham Green.

Leighton House Museum & Art Gallery W14
12 Holland Park Rd   (020) 7602 3316   1–3B
No visitor to Holland Park should miss this extraordinary mid-Victorian house, with later Moorish Hall (complete with small pool). It is a wonderful setting for the permanent collection of paintings by Frederic, Lord Leighton (1830–96) and some of his contemporaries. In summer, the garden, which contains some sculptures, is open. There are also temporary exhibitions in the recently refurbished Perrin Gallery – if you want to assess current standards in what was once London's most famous artistic quarter, don't miss the Kensington and Chelsea Artists' Show in July. / Times: Wed-Mon 11am-5.30pm; www.rbkc.gov.uk/leightonhousemuseum/general/; Tube: High Street Kensington.

Lindsey House SW10
99-100 Cheyne Walk   (01494) 528051 (National Trust)
3–3C
Overlooking the Thames, this building dates from 1674 and is on the site of Sir Thomas More's garden. Despite being owned by the National Trust, it is tenanted, so sightseeing is by appointment only (via the Trust's regional office on the number given) and only on four selected dates per year. Visits are restricted to the ground floor entrance hall, main staircase, first floors and gardens, but you can admire the splendid c17 exterior at any time. / www.nationaltrust.org.uk; Tube: Sloane Square or South Kensington (both around 1.5 miles away).

Narwhal Inuit Art Gallery W4
55 Linden Gardens   (020) 8742 1268   1–3A
A gallery with an unusual theme – Inuit (Eskimo) art of Canada, Russia, Alaska and Greenland. The culture dates back 15,000 years, and, even though there is no Inuit word for 'art', the collection includes sculptures, prints, wall hangings, ceramics, woven baskets, embroidery, carvings and graphics. View by prior appointment only. / www.niaef.com; Tube: Turnham Green; Café, Restaurant, Picnic area.

National Army Museum SW3
Royal Hospital Rd   (020) 7730 0717   3–3D
The Army's own museum relates its history, from the archers of Henry V to involvement in contemporary UN peacekeeping operations. The emphasis is on the story of the individual soldier – the "human aspect". There is a major collection of uniforms, life-sized models in costumes through the ages, paintings of famous battle scenes, portraits by Reynolds and Gainsborough and displays of weaponry and medals, as well as some interactive aspects – visitors are welcome to try on helmets and play with the dioramas. A visit here makes a good fit with a trip to the neighbouring Royal Hospital (see also). / Times: 10am-5.30pm; www.national-army-museum.ac.uk; Tube: Sloane Square.

Natural History Museum SW7
Cromwell Rd   (020) 7938 9123   3–2C
*Access to this huge and impressive South Kensington museum
is now, once again, entirely free (so arrive early – at weekends
and on holidays, key sections soon fill up). There's an incredible
amount to see, with exhibits drawn from a collection of 78
million specimens, ranging from a 26-metre Diplodocus to a
segment from the trunk of a 1,300 million year-old sequoia.
You will want to spend a few minutes in the cathedral-like
central hall, before taking in the Dinosaurs exhibition – a
recent addition to the dinosaur pit is a fearsome, robotic,
Tyrannosaurus rex, who not only moves and roars, but also
smells realistic! You might also like to find out how your body
works, by visiting the Human Biology Gallery. The museum has
many interactive displays – it even offers the possibility of
'experiencing' the Kobe earthquake (as felt inside a
supermarket) – and is most definitely worth a return visit or
two.* / Times: 10am-5.50pm, Sun 11am-5.50pm; www.nhm.ac.uk; Tube: South
Kensington; Café, Restaurant, Picnic area.

The Orangery & the Ice House W8
Holland Park   (020) 7603 1123   3–1A
*The charming c18 glasshouse in the centre of Holland Park
and the nearby Ice House are used for five high-quality arts
and crafts exhibitions in various media every year. Call for
further information on exhibitions and hours in operation.*
/ Times: 11am-7pm (during exhibitions); www.rbkc.gov.uk/theorangery;
Tube: High Street Kensington, Holland Park; Café.

Orleans House Gallery, Middx
Riverside, Twickenham   (020) 8831 6000
*Twickenham benefits from an unusually attractive gallery in
which to display its borough art collection and to hold
contemporary art exhibitions (around five annually). It was
designed by James Gibbs in 1720, as the garden pavilion of a
very grand house (itself demolished two centuries later) and is
richly decorated with ornamental mouldings and gilt. The
setting, in a picturesque woodland garden by the Thames (open
daylight hours), is a good place for a picnic or as a starting
point for a stroll along the river. During the summer (Apr-Oct),
one can also visit the Stables Gallery, which holds frequently-
changing exhibitions.* / Times: Tue-Sat 1pm-5.30pm (Oct-Mar 4.30pm),
Sun & bank hols 2pm-5.30pm (Oct-Mar 4.30pm); www.richmond.gov.uk;
Tube: Richmond or BR: St Margarets (closer than tube); Picnic area.

Pitzhanger Manor House W5
Mattock Ln (020) 8567 1227 1–3A
*This Ealing house, set in a park, already had the benefit of
some exquisite plaster work designed by George Dance in the
mid-c18, when it attracted the attentions of the great neo-
classical architect, Sir John Soane. Between 1800 and 1810,
he transformed the house into a Regency villa for himself and
his family. The building (Grade I listed, and open to the public
since 1987) merits a visit in its own right. The house is also
home to the Hull Grundy Bequest, the largest public collection
of Martinware – the Victorian art pottery made by the four
Martin brothers of Southall between 1877 and 1923 – in the
country. The brothers were best known for their bird sculptures
and bowls, vessels adorned with sea creatures, and tiles,
designed in a capricious but highly-skilled style. (Much of
Southall Library's collection of Martinware has recently been
re-housed here, too.) There's also an art gallery with changing
exhibitions of contemporary art.* / Times: Tue-Sat 11am-5pm;
www.ealing.gov.uk; Tube: Ealing Broadway; Café.

Polish Institute & Sikorsi Museum SW7
20 Princes Gate (020) 7589 9249 3–1C
*Anyone with even a passing interest in Poland or in military
history should visit this elegant museum near Hyde Park –
it is by far the most important collection of Polish material
anywhere outside that country. There are important
momentoes of the many conflicts in which Poles have been
involved – including the national flag flown over the ruins of the
monastery of Monte Cassino in 1944. The archives contain
around two million documents, as well as other materials from
the Polish Government and Polish Embassies around the world,
mostly from WWII (when they came to London, rather than to
the Communist Government in Poland). A photograph and film
archive is also available for viewing.* / Times: Mon-Fri 2pm-4pm; 1st
Sat of month 10am-4pm; archives Tue-Fri 9.30am-4pm; Tube: South
Kensington, Knightsbridge.

Royal College of Art SW7
Kensington Gore (020) 7590 4444 3–1B
*This is the only exclusively post-graduate university of art and
design in the world – famous graduates include David
Hockney, Henry Moore and Barbara Hepworth. Courses range
from painting, through fashion, to vehicle design and curating.
There's almost always an exhibition in progress and most are
free – but call the Public Relations office on (020) 7590 4121
before you set out to avoid disappointment.* / Times: during
exhibitions, Mon-Fri 10am-6pm; www.rca.ac.uk; Tube: Knightsbridge, South
Kensington, High Street Kensington.

Royal College of Music – Department of Portraits & Performance History SW7

Prince Consort Rd   (020) 7591 4340   3–1B

Owing to space constraints the college is not – as we go to press – able to display its collection of portraits and busts of c19 and early c20 musicians (housed in a sixth floor gallery, to which there is no lift). This situation may change in 2004. (The college also has a museum displaying its collection of rare instruments which is open, for which there is a small charge). / Times: Portrait Collection, when in operation, Mon-Fri 10am-5.30pm by telephone appointment; Museum Wed 2pm-4.30pm during term time, except January; www.rcm.ac.uk; Tube: South Kensington, Gloucester Road.

The Royal Hospital Chelsea SW3

Royal Hospital Rd   (020) 7730 5282   3–3D

Wren's elegant 1682 building, founded by Charles II for veteran soldiers, is still the home of the Chelsea Pensioners, who can sometimes be spotted around the area wearing their splendid scarlet uniforms. Indeed, give two weeks' notice and a tour, guided by one of the pensioners, can be arranged. The Great Hall, the Chapel and the Museum may be visited. Don't miss the lovely grounds, Ranelagh Gardens (see also). / Times: Mon-Sat 10am-12pm & 2pm-4pm; www.chelseapensioner.org.uk; Tube: Sloane Square; Café, Restaurant, Picnic area.

Royal Military School of Music, Middx

Kneller Hall, Kneller Rd, Twickenham   (020) 8898 5533

This collection of instruments used by the military includes wind and stringed items from the past three centuries. Of particular interest, perhaps, is a bugle played at the Battle of Waterloo and indigenous percussion instruments, including 'talking drums' from Africa. Tours can include a visit to the Chapel and the museum, and hearing a band in rehearsal. / Times: by written appointment, generally Wed mornings Jun-Aug; BR: Whitton; Café.

Science Museum SW7

Exhibition Rd   (08708) 704771   3–1C

Appropriately for the prime technological museum of the first industrial nation, the 200,000 exhibits contain many 'firsts' – the first steam engine of the c18 and the first steam turbine of the c19, Stephenson's train (the Rocket) and the Vickers Vimy aircraft which made the first non-stop Atlantic crossing in 1919. Many attractions are more contemporary, including the Apollo 10 spacecraft, still scorched from re-entry into the atmosphere. There's always a great deal going on throughout the museum, and there are enough 'hands-on' exhibits in the 40 galleries to keep children from as young as three happy. Six new interactive galleries, ranging from digital technology to genetics, were recently added. There are charges for some special exhibitions. / Times: 10.00am-6.00pm seven days; www.sciencemuseum.org.uk; Tube: South Kensington; Café.

Serpentine Gallery W2

Kensington Gardens   (020) 7298 1515 info line   3–1C
*The attractive and popular Hyde Park gallery re-opened in
February 1998 after a major renovation. It stages a number of
modern and contemporary exhibitions annually of artists from
around the globe. There are usually talks by artists and critics
on Saturday afternoons at 3pm. / Times: 10am-6pm;*
www.serpentinegallery.org; Tube: Lancaster Gate, South Kensington; Café.

Victoria & Albert Museum* SW7

Cromwell Rd   0870 442 0808, (020) 7942 2000   3–2C
*Founded in 1852, the "world's largest decorative arts and
design museum" comprises over 145 galleries, reflecting
centuries of artistic achievement from Europe, the Far East,
South East Asia and the Islamic world. There are extensive
collections of ceramics, furniture, jewellery and dress, from
ancient times to the present day. The V & A has been
undergoing some well-needed redevelopment in the last couple
of years. This includes the new British Galleries (opened in
2001) where the collection has been re-displayed as fifteen
new galleries telling the story of British design and decorative
art from 1500-1900. The galleries include some 3,000
exhibits, enhanced by interactive computers, video screens and
audio programmes. Also the English silver galleries were finally
finished in 2002, and contain over 1200 objects, dating from
1300-1800. Other star attractions include a collection of
Raphael's seven tapestry cartoons – preparatory designs for
tapestries – depicting the acts of Christ's apostles. The
cartoons, claimed among the greatest artistic treasures in
Britain, were originally commissioned by Pope Leo XI for the
Sistine Chapel. / Times: Mon-Sun 10am-5.45pm (Wed & last Fri of the
month 10pm); www.vam.ac.uk; Tube: South Kensington; Café, Restaurant.*

William Morris Society W6

Kelmscott House, 26 Upper Mall   (020) 8741 3735   1–3A
*Occupying part of the house in which Morris – socialist,
designer and author – lived from 1878 until his death in 1896,
this small collection of memorabilia, designs and books includes
one of the original presses on which his novels, poetry and
pamphlets were printed. (Devotees should also see the entry
for the William Morris Gallery in the East End section.)*

/ Times: Thu & Sat 2pm-5pm; www.morrissociety.org; Tube: Ravenscourt Park.

Outdoor attractions

Albert Memorial SW7
Prince's Gate, Kensington Gore   3–1B
*The Albert Memorial – after refurbishment – can now be seen
in all its gilded splendour. The memorial was conceived in
1852, to celebrate the Great Exhibition (the Crystal Palace
having just been dismantled and removed from Hyde Park),
and was to feature a statue of Victoria's consort, Prince Albert.
However, his death in 1861 (years before completion of the
monument) changed the focus completely. It is decorated with
nearly 200 statues representing the arts, sciences, industries,
continents and moral virtues, while the frieze of Parnassus
depicts 169 life-size figures of the world's artistic genii. (The
Prince hated the idea that his statue should be placed in the
memorial – "it would disturb my quiet rides in Rotten Row to
see my own face staring at me.")* / Tube: Knightsbridge, South
Kensington.

Bayswater Road Market W2
Bayswater Rd   1–2B
*Wander along the north edge of Kensington Gardens on a
Sunday afternoon, and seemingly every piece of railing is
covered with temporary pitches of artists hawking their wares.
Amongst the cheesy canvasses designed to woo dewy-eyed
tourists you can find some surprisingly good pieces of work –
as well as paintings and sketches, there are also generally
sculptures and handmade jewellery.* / Times: Sundays 10am-6pm;
Tube, Bus: Lancaster Gate, Queensway.

Brent Lodge Park W7
Church Rd, Hanwell   (020) 8566 1929   1–2A
*Once known as 'the bunny park' because of its teeming rabbit
population, this expansive area – some 800 acres – has wide
open spaces surrounded by dense pockets of trees, and makes
a good destination for a quiet picnic or a family day out. The
river Brent crosses directly through the park, and there are a
number of small bridges connecting the two sections. There is
an animal centre (part of which has an entry charge) housing
guinea pigs, rabbits and pheasants, to name a few of the furry
creatures you might encounter there. The Millennium Maze is
the newly growing, new attraction* / Times: 7am-dusk;
www.ealing.gov.uk/Parks; BR: Hanwell or 207 bus or E1 or E3 buses; Café,
Picnic area.

Burnham Beeches, Bucks
Farnham Common   (01753) 647358
Though not quite IN London, this famous beauty spot – one of the finest examples of ancient woodland in Britain – can fairly claim to be OF the capital city as it has been owned by the Corporation of London since 1880. The most famous feature of the 540-acre site is the beech pollards, some of which are almost 500 years old. There is a programme of regular free walks and talks, and usually an annual open day in late June (check the website or call for details). The latter offers a chance to see displays of falconry, countryside management techniques and examples of country crafts. Given the wood's accessibility (just north of Junction 6 of the M4), it would be the perfect place to get away from it all if it were not for the fact that every year half a million other people have the same idea! Autumn is the very best time to visit.
/ *Times: pedestrians 24 hours; vehicles 8am-one hour after sunset; www.cityoflondon.gov.uk; BR: Slough (then bus to Farnham Common).*

Bushy Park, Middx
White Lodge, The Stockyard, Bushy Park,
Hampton Court Rd, Hampton Hill   (020) 8979 1586
This ancient deer park was laid out as part of Wren's grand design for neighbouring Hampton Court. Herds of red and fallow deer roam its 1,100 acres. The Woodland Gardens, with their fine azaleas, camellias and rhododendrons, are a post-war addition and make a nice place for a picnic. They boast a fine chestnut avenue which is the focal point of Chestnut Sunday – this a traditional Victorian parade and picnic, which takes place every other year in May and celebrates the blossoming of the trees. / *Times: 6.30am-dusk summer (7pm winter); www.royalparks.gov.uk; BR: Hampton Wick.*

Chelsea Antiques Market SW3
245-253 Kings Rd   3–3C
If you love nothing more than browsing among bric-a-brac and antiques, this is the place for you. In the heart of Chelsea, this characterful arcade is packed with stalls brimming with all sorts of collectables, including books and jewellery in a wide variety of styles. / *Times: Mon-Sat 10am-6pm; Tube, Bus: Sloane Square.*

Chelsea Harbour SW10
(020) 7225 9100   3–4B
This contemporary riverside marina development never seems to have lived up to its aspirations, but makes a pleasant place for a riverside walk. (Despite its relatively central location, the Harbour has a surprisingly far-away feel and – on a good day and with a little bit of imagination – is about as close as London gets to the French Riviera.) Reflecting the proximity of many of London's grander residential areas, the development has become a centre for interior design firms. They are largely 'trade only', but there is an annual open day in March, highlighting new trends in interior design.
/ *www.chelsea-harbour.co.uk; Tube: Earl's Court (then C3 bus).*

Chiswick House* W4

Burlington Ln   (020) 8995 5390   1–3A

*The mainly wooded, 64-acre gardens of this fine neo-classical
villa have suitably Italianate highlights – statues, temples, urns
and obelisks – and there is also a lake and a cascade waterfall.
There is a picnic area (and also a café). The house (to which
there is an entry charge) is run by English Heritage.* / Times: park
8am-dusk (approx 5.15pm in winter, 9.30pm in summer); information centre
9am-30 minutes before the park closes; www.english-heritage.org.uk;
Tube: Turnham Green (then E3 bus); Café.

Crane Park Island, Middx

Crane Park, Twickenham   (020) 7261 0447

*This small island (just over four acres), accessed by bridge, has
its place in history – the old gunpowder mill here (now
demolished) is believed to have been where Guy Fawkes
obtained his supplies. Nowadays, its attractions are more
peaceful, and it's an agreeable site, run by the London Wildlife
Trust. Due to the cleanliness of its water, it is home to the rare
water vole, and also safe for kids to paddle in. There are also
three paths, one of which (the Hobbin Path) is suitable for
disabled people. During the summer holidays, there is a
playscheme – call for details.* / Times: 24 hours;
www.wildlondon.org.uk/; BR: Whitton.

Garrick's Temple & Lawn at Hampton

Hampton Court Rd   (020) 8892 0221 (Orleans House
Gallery), (020) 8255 4903 (Hampton Riverside Trust)

*This garden building on the Thames, a 10 minute walk from
Hampton Court Palace, was built in 1755-6 by David Garrick
– England's second most famous actor, dramatist and theatre
manager – to commemorate his idol, William Shakespeare.
After a recent restoration, the opportunity was taken to install
a display traversing Garrick's acting career and his Hampton
private life.* / Times: Temple: April-Sept. Sundays 2pm-5pm and by appt.;
Lawn: Daily throughout the year 7.30am-dusk;
www.richmond.gov.uk/orleanshouse; BR: Hampton Court and then R68 bus or
Hampton and then 111 or 216 bus.

Gunnersbury Triangle Nature Reserve W4

Bollo Ln   (020) 8747 3881   1–3A

*This six-acre site developed a rich covering of vegetation after
being surrounded by railway tracks in the late c19. Since then it
has been undisturbed, apart from some allotments, until it was
threatened by development in the early '80s and became a
'test case'. The conservationists won, and this was the first time
that a planning inspector had preferred nature conservation to
development on a city site. It is now managed by the local
volunteers of the London Wildlife Trust and during summer
school holidays there is a usually a full-time warden (daily) and
a programme of free events. There is also a small information
centre.* / Times: Tue 10am-4pm, Fri & Sun 2pm-4.30pm; also some Sats &
school hols; www.chiswickw4.com; Tube: Chiswick Park.

Hampton Court Palace Gardens*, Middx
0870 752 7777

The wonderful gardens and park of Wolsey's great riverside palace (completed by Henry VIII and substantially altered by William and Mary) are open to the public without charge, and the formal gardens are the most visited free attraction of their type in the country. They include features from Victorian times, as well as from the earlier periods of the palace's construction, and a riverside walk. Around the gardens, in the 560-acre area that includes both Bushey and Home parks, graze the descendants of the deer hunted by Tudor monarchs. There is a charge for access to the Palace itself, the maze and the Privy Garden of William III. / Times: 8am-dusk; www.hrp.org.uk; BR: Hampton Court; Café.

Holland Park W8
Ilchester Place   (020) 7602 9483   1–3B

Until some forty years ago, Holland Park was an extraordinary hangover from former days – a private 'country' estate, in the middle of London. It maintains a unique and charming character, and, in spite of its relatively small size (52 acres), some of it is heavily wooded (and managed so as to enhance wildlife). Apart from its superb formal gardens, it benefits from the Kyoto Garden, installed by Japanese benefactors in 1991. Visit just before sunset to witness the peacocks' bedtime, when the birds fly into the trees and screech to one another. Other attractions include a large adventure playground and the Ecology Centre, which has a series of free talks. There are also educational events for organised groups (details from the Ecology Service) including pond dipping for children, and a conservation programme for volunteers of all ages. The Park contains the Orangery and the Ice House (see also). / Times: 7.30am-30 mins before dusk 7 days a week; www.rbkc.gov.uk; Tube: Holland Park, Kensington High Street; Café.

Hyde Park W2
(020) 7298 2000   3–1C

The greatest of the central Royal Parks was originally acquired by Henry VIII from the Abbey at Westminster as a private hunting ground. In 1637, when Charles I opened it to the public, it became notorious as a haunt of footpads and thieves. (William III later had 300 oil lamps erected to deter them, creating Britain's first artificially-lit highway.) The giant glass structure of Crystal Palace covered almost eight hectares of the park when it was erected for the Great Exhibition of 1851.

The park's 344 acres now offer a variety of attractions, ranging from the formal gardens along its south side, Rotten Row (a bridleway for more than 300 years, its name derived from the French 'Route du Roi'), a river (the Serpentine) and areas of woods and grass. There is a children's playground and a Pet Cemetery (open only one day a year in Sept; look for posters around the park advertising the date). In summer, there are weekend and bank holiday concerts at the bandstand (afternoons and evenings). Speakers' Corner (see also) is situated in the north east corner of the park. Kensington Gardens (see also) adjoin the park, and many more attractions can be found there. / Times: 5am-12am; www.royalparks.gov.uk; Tube: Knightsbridge, Hyde Park Corner, Marble Arch, Lancaster Gate, Queensway; Café, Picnic area.

Kensington Gardens W2
(020) 7298 2117   3–1B
These were the private gardens of Kensington Palace (designed by Wren) and were largely laid out under the direction of Queen Caroline in 1728. The gardens were opened to the public by Queen Victoria and are effectively an extension of Hyde Park (see also). Attractions in the 275 acres include the Round Pond for boating (model boats only, please) where the Model Boat Club meets every Sunday morning, the charming small statue of Peter Pan and the very pretty area in the immediate vicinity of the Palace itself. The gardens also house the Serpentine Gallery and the Albert Memorial (see also). In 2000, the Diana Memorial Playground replaced one of the original playgrounds. It is based on a Peter Pan theme and is open 10am-dusk. In summer, there are weekly concerts at the bandstand, occasional country dancing displays and children's entertainments. / Times: dawn-dusk; www.royalparks.gov.uk; Tube: Bayswater, Lancaster Gate, Queensway, High Street Kensington; Café.

Kensington Roof Gardens W8
Barkers Department Store, Kensington High St (entrance 99 Derry St)   (020) 7937 7994   3–1A
Opened in the 1930s, this extraordinary 6th-floor installation is Europe's largest roof garden (1.5 acres), and is most certainly worth a visit. It is now home to a nightclub owned by Sir Richard Branson, but (subject to prior club commitments) daytime visitors are welcome. There are in fact three themed adjoining gardens – an English woodland garden with flamingos, a Tudor garden and a Spanish garden with palm trees. / Times: 11am-5pm, but call first; www.roofgardens.com; Tube: High Street Kensington.

Marble Hill House*, Middx
Richmond Rd, Twickenham   (020) 8892 5115
Built in the 1720s as a retreat from court life for Henrietta Howard, Countess of Suffolk (George II's mistress), this Palladian villa – one of the most perfect surviving examples of the type – inhabits a park of 60 acres which stretches down to the river. There is an admission charge for the house, but access to the grounds is free. / Times: dawn-dusk; www.guidetorichmond.co.uk/marblehill.html; Tube: Richmond; Café.

North End Road Market SW6
North End Rd   (020) 8748 3020   3–4A
Its not the loveliest stretch of road in Fulham, but there's something grittily atmospheric about this large, haphazard street market selling fruit, veg and bric-a-brac – one of the largest in West London. At weekends the crush is so great it can be difficult to make headway along the pavement. / Times: Mon-Sat 9am-5pm, Sun 9.30am-12.30pm; Tube, Bus: Fulham Broadway.

Osterley Park*, Middx
Isleworth   (020) 8568 7714
This is one of the last great houses with an intact estate in Greater London, set in 140 acres of landscaped park and farmland with ornamental lakes. Originally a c16 mansion (built for Sir Thomas Gresham, founder of the Royal Exchange), it was transformed into neo-classical style by Robert Adam in the c18. Though the house has been a National Trust property for over half a century, the trust only took over the management in 1990 (and both the grounds and garden house have recently been refurbished). There is a charge for admission to the house although access to the Jersey galleries is free. These galleries house temporary exhibitions of contemporary and local art. Entrance is through the house so you get a glimpse of the interior free of charge! / Times: park 9am-7.30pm or sunset if earlier; www.nationaltrust.org.uk; Tube: Osterley; Café.

Portobello Road Market W10, W11
1–2B
On Saturday, Portobello market is undoubtedly the place in West London for combining people-watching and browsing. The street market stretches for over a mile, and in fact comprises several different markets. The most famous, the antiques market, is at the south end, but there is also a food market, bric-à-brac stalls and (under the Westway) a good gathering of vendors of trendy clothing and accessories.
/ www.portobelloroad.co.uk; Tube: Notting Hill Gate, Ladbroke Grove.

Ranelagh Gardens SW3
Royal Hospital Rd   3–3D
Apart from when they are cordoned off every year (in May) for the famous Chelsea Flower Show, these well-kept gardens lead a rather low-profile life. They are, however, unusually pretty and intimate. A visit here combines well with one to the neighbouring Royal Hospital (see also). / Times: 10am (Sun 2pm)-30 mins before dusk, closed 1pm-2pm; Tube: Sloane Square.

Riverside Walk
See the introduction of the South section for suggestions of interesting walks by the Thames.

Ruislip Woods, Middx

Ruislip   (01895) 250635

There are a number of noteworthy features of these 700 acres of woodland, including the 250-acre Park Wood, the largest unbroken stretch of woodland in London. A particular attraction is the barbecue sites located in the Bayhurst Wood Country Park, another portion of the woods: although there is a charge to book these, you don't have to pay if you are prepared to take pot luck. Ruislip Woodland Centre covers the history of the area, which became a National Nature Reserve in 1997. The centre also gives details of the various species inhabiting the area – there are bats (at dawn and dusk), woodpeckers, warblers and woodcocks to name a few. A short guide to Ruislip Woods is available in local libraries or from the Leisure Service, Education, Youth and Leisure Department, Civic Centre, Uxbridge, Middx UB8 1UW. / Times: woodland centre Sat & Sun 12pm-3.30pm; www.hillingdon.gov.uk; Tube: Ruislip (then 331 bus); Café.

Shepherd's Bush Market W12

Runs between Uxbridge Rd and Goldhawk Rd   1–3B

Stretched out at the foot of and in the arches of the Hammersmith & City line between Goldhawk Road and Shepherd's Bush stations, this long narrow market (as popularised by Domestic Goddess, Nigella Lawson, in her former life) sells a wide variety of goods, fabrics and foods – most of it pretty cheaply. There are over 300 stalls and shops, and the heady mix of different Asian and African foodstuffs in some sections can create an exotic atmosphere even in this most urban of locations. / Times: Tues, Wed, Fri, Sat 9am-5pm, Sun 8.30am-3pm; Tube, Bus: Shepherds Bush.

North London

Introduction

North London's unique strength is the way it contains pockets of real nature, which seem to be only a stone's throw from the metropolis itself. The most obvious example is **Hampstead Heath**, but there is also **Highgate Wood** – and both are accessible by foot from the **Parkland Walk**, see also – and each is within a few tube stops of anywhere in central London.

In addition, there are many fine parks in the area. North London has its own Royal Park, in the form of **Regent's Park**, and its extension to the North, **Primrose Hill**, which has exceptional views over the city. **Alexandra Palace Park** gives yet another impressive perspective on the city below. The grounds of **Golders Green Crematorium** are a surprisingly fine amenity, relatively unknown to those outside the locality.

Few would dispute that Hampstead is by far the finest village in London, and two of its lovely period houses may be visited – **Burgh House** (whose museum gives the history of the area) and Keats House. The village's grandest residence, **Kenwood House**, at the top of the Heath, has an excellent period art collection.

For people who like being among people, the undoubted attraction is colourful **Camden Market**, which, every weekend, sprawls over the area from the Lock to the tube station. For children, it's probably the green spaces and the nature which are the main plus points. For the more inquisitive, however, the **Wellcome Trust's** exhibitions (including the **Two10 Gallery**) offer an interesting diversion.

Brent One Stop Shop
Brent Town Hall, Forty Ln   Customer Call Centre (020) 8937 1200   1–*1A*
/ Times: Mon-Fri 9am-5pm; www.brent.gov.uk; Tube: Wembly Park.

Camden Direct Information Centre NW3
3-5 Cressy Rd (postal enquiries only)   (020) 7974 5974
Free tourist and travel information on London as well as local information about Camden / www.cindex.camden.gov.uk; Tube: Kings Cross; Café, Restaurant, Picnic area.

Harrow Tourist Information Centre, Middx
The Civic Centre, Station Rd, Harrow   (020) 8424 1103
The centre provides detailed information concerning local history, specific places of interest and nature preserves in Harrow. Local maps also are available. / Times: Mon-Fri 9am-5pm; www.harrow.gov.uk; BR: Harrow & Wealdstone.

Suggested walk

For a taste of the varied nature of North London, set
out for a stroll beginning in Regent's Park at the point
where it meets the northern end of Baker Street. Head
north – there are maps to guide you – and you will cross
the entire width of the park, passing the boating lake to
your left, Queen Mary's Gardens and the Zoo. Exiting
the main northern entrance of the park, cross Regent's
Canal and join Regent's Park Road. This winds along
Primrose Hill, offering majestic views of London, as well
as of stately houses and tree-lined streets. Continue
walking until you reach Chalk Farm Road, with its array
of eclectic shops and restaurants. Follow the road south
– the activity increases as you reach Camden Lock and,
at weekends, the bustling market. If the crowds prove
too daunting, sneak down from the bridge at Camden
Lock to Regent's Canal and walk east a mile or so to
Camley Street Nature Park.

Indoor attractions

Barnet Museum, Herts
31 Wood St, Barnet   (020) 8440 8066
*Wide-ranging local history museum whose three or four annual
temporary exhibits include shields from the Battle of Barnet –
the penultimate battle in the Wars of the Roses. / Times: Tue-Thu
2.30pm-4.30pm, Sat 10.30am-12.30pm & 2pm-4pm; Tube: High Barnet (then
a half mile walk or 184 bus).*

Batchworth Lock Canal Centre, Herts
99 Church St, Rickmansworth   (01923) 778382
*Batchworth Lock is an historic site on the Grand Union Canal.
Located in former stables, the centre provides guides, leaflets
and maps showing the network of waterways around
Batchworth. One can visit the narrow boats 'Albert' and
'Roger', and even enjoy a 30 minute return trip on the canal to
Stockers Lock. Donations are appreciated. / Times: Easter
weekend-end Oct Mon, Thur, Fri 10am-3pm, Sat & Sun 11am-5pm;
www.hertsmuseums.org.uk/info/batchworth.htm; Tube: Rickmansworth.*

British Library NW1
96 Euston Rd   (020) 7412 7000   4–3C
*Does it look like an academy for secret policemen? That was
the Prince of Wales's opinion on this striking building, home to
every book published in the UK. You too can form a view of the
architecture from the courtyard, but most of the library itself is
reserved for those with reader cards. There are, however, two*

permanent exhibition galleries. The John Ritblat Gallery exhibits over 200 items, including Magna Carta, the Lindisfarne Gospels and a Gutenberg Bible. The second is the Workshop of Words, Sound and Images, an interactive gallery that follows book production from the earliest written documents to the digital revolution of our time. On Saturdays, there are free demonstrations of bookbinding, calligraphy and printing.
/ Times: Mon, Wed & Fri 9.30am-6pm, Tue 9.30am-8pm, Sat 9.30am-5pm & Sun and bank holidays 11am-5pm; www.bl.uk; Tube: Kings Cross.

Bruce Castle Museum N17
Lordship Ln   (020) 8808 8772
Haringey's museum, with its wide collection of items of local interest, occupies an elegant and striking Grade I listed Tudor manor house. It was also once a school run by a Mr Hill and his sons (one of whom was called Roland), which operated on progressive lines (for its day) – for example, there was no corporal punishment and the children were involved in its administration. Roland Hill grew up to be the inventor of the uniformed penny post – a postal history collection reflects his connection with the house. Bruce Castle is located in two acres of parkland, containing a children's playground, bowling green, tennis court and basketball area. An interactive centre has recently been added. Sun 2pm-4pm, there are family activities, and the last Wed evening of each month, there are free talks and events (at 7pm). Past events have included a celebration of Goan culture and a talk about the archaeology of a local farm. Temporary art exhibitions are held from time to time, and during the summer, there are regular arts and crafts activities.
/ Times: Wed-Fri 1pm-5pm, Sat & Sun 10am-5pm; www.haringey.gov.uk/data/brucecastle/index.asp; Tube: Wood Green (then 243 bus).

Burgh House & Hampstead Museum NW3
New End Sq   (020) 7431 0144   4–1A
This handsome Queen Anne house (1703) is well worth a visit for its architecture, its pictures and its creaking charm. The ground floor is used as a community centre for the arts and houses temporary art exhibitions. The museum is on the first floor and has displays and objects about the history of Hampstead (long regarded as one of the most desirable places to live in or near the capital) and changing exhibitions on the history of the area. The house makes an ideal stopping-off point between the tube station and the Heath, and in the summer there is a nice garden to admire. / Times: Wed-Sun (& bank hols) 12pm-5pm; Tube: Hampstead; Café.

Camden Arts Centre NW3
Arkwright Rd   (020) 7604 4504   4–2A
The centre's three galleries hold about half a dozen contemporary art exhibitions a year. During shows, there are usually artist-led Sunday talks every two to three weeks. (Note, as we go to press the centre is closed for major refurbishment – till late 2003 – and its telephone number may change).
/ Times: Tue-Thu 11am-7pm, Fri-Sun 11am-5.30pm; www.camdenartscentre.org; Tube: Finchley Road.

Church Farmhouse Museum* NW4
Greyhound Hill   (020) 8203 0130
Built in 1660, this charming listed building (Hendon's oldest dwelling) combines permanent displays of c19 life with temporary exhibitions on local and social history and the decorative arts (and in December to February each year there's an exhibition especially for children). It has three reconstructed period rooms: kitchen (c1820); laundry room (c1890) and dining room (c1850). (The dining room is decorated for a Victorian Christmas every December). / Times: Mon-Thu 10am-12.30pm & 1.30pm-5pm, Sat 10am-1pm & 2pm-5.30pm, Sun 2pm-5.30pm; www.barnet.gov.uk/cultural_services/museums; Tube: Hendon Central; Café, Restaurant, Picnic area.

Crafts Council N1
44a Pentonville Rd   (020) 7278 7700   4–3D
The council is the national body for promoting contemporary crafts, such as pottery, textiles and printing. Its premises include picture and reference libraries as well as a gallery. There are five major exhibitions a year – retrospectives of major artisans or thematic shows of contemporary craft, and there are related events (workshops, lectures, demonstrations) in conjunction with the exhibitions. Recent highlights include exhibitions on weird and wacky spectacles and on contemporary jewellery made in Britain. There is also an information service relating to contemporary British crafts. / Times: Tue-Sun 11am (Sun 2pm)-6pm; www.craftscouncil.org.uk; Tube: Angel.

Grange Museum of Community History NW10
Neasden Roundabout, Neasden Ln   (020) 8452 8311
1–1A
Brent's community museum, in a converted c18 cottage, includes an Edwardian draper's shop (transplanted from Willesden High Road) and a Victorian Parlour. A permanent exhibition, 'The Brent People', includes a computerised database of local photographs. There is a temporary exhibition space, the Community Gallery, that shows about three or four exhibitions a year. Two computers are set up for free Internet browsing. This is a child-friendly museum, with 'The Space' (which contains a mystery hat and other odd bits for dressing-up), an enclosed garden (with Victorian herb border) open for picnicking, and children's shows, events and activities in the summer. / Times: Mon-Sat 11am (Sat 10am)-5pm (also Sun 2pm-5pm in August); www.brent.gov.uk; Tube: Neasden; Picnic area.

Harrow Museum & Heritage Centre, Middx
Headstone Manor, Pinner View, Harrow   (020) 8861 2626
Originally built for the c14 Archbishops of Canterbury, this moated manor house has '30s interiors which are still in the course of renovation. It benefits from a pretty setting in a park, and there is also a c18 granary and a large and interesting c16 tithe barn. Here, a Victorian room setting, changing exhibitions and local history displays are on view, and there are lunchtime concerts on Sunday. / Times: Thu-Sat 12.30pm-5pm, Sun & Bank Holidays 10.30am-5pm; www.harrowarts.com; Tube: Harrow-on-the-Hill (then H10 or H14 bus); Café, Picnic area.

North London

Islington Museum Gallery N1
Foyer Gallery, Town Hall, Upper St   (020) 7527 3235
4–2D
*It is surprising that Islington – which has undergone a
transformation from notorious slum to 'in' part of the capital
(forever associated in the public mind with the rise of New
Labour) – lacks a fully-fledged local museum. However, in the
interim, this volunteer-run gallery is the setting for about five
exhibitions a year, exploring the history, sociology, ethnic
culture, artistic heritage and architecture of the area.*
/ Times: Wed-Sat 11am-5pm, Sun 2pm-4pm; www.islington.gov.uk/localinfo;
Tube: Highbury & Islington.

Kenwood House NW3
Hampstead Ln   (020) 8348 1286   4–1A
*Perched like a grand wedding cake above Hampstead Heath,
this neo-classical house (with Robert Adam façade, 1760s)
provides a great cultural climax to a visit to the heath. The
house (which was bequeathed to the nation by the first Earl of
Iveagh in 1926) is certainly worth a view (the library is
reckoned to be one of Adam's finest rooms), as are the artistic
treasures within, which include a Rembrandt self-portrait and
Vermeer's Guitar Player, as well as many famous works by
Turner, Reynolds, Gainsborough, Van Dyck and Frans Hals. If
you wander the paths on the estate, you might chance upon
sculptures by Henry Moore and Barbara Hepworth. In the
summer, open air concerts are held in the bowl by the lake –
you can hear them from outside the pay-to-enter enclosure.*
/ Times: Mar-Sep 10am-6pm, Oct 10am-5pm, Nov-Mar 10am-4pm;
www.english-heritage.org.uk; Tube: Archway or Golders Green (then 210 bus);
Café.

Lauderdale House Community Arts Centre* N6
Waterlow Park, Highgate Hill   (020) 8348 8716   1–1C
*The three galleries of this Elizabethan house set in the centre
of the attractive Waterlow Park hold frequently changing
exhibitions. The centre holds regular performances (jazz,
cabaret, classical concerts and children's shows), workshops,
fairs and family events. Entry to the house and galleries is free
except when special exhibitions are held. Most shows and
workshops are free, although occasionally a fee is charged, so
it's generally best to call before you travel.* / Times: Tue-Fri
11am-4pm, Sat 1.30pm-5pm, Sun 12pm-5pm (weekends subject to private
booking); www.london-northwest.com/lauderdalearts; Tube: Archway (then 143,
210 or 271 bus); Café.

London International Gallery of Children's Art NW3
255 Finchley Rd   (020) 7435 0903   1–1B
*London's only gallery devoted to children's art from around the
world. You can check out the current show on their website.*
/ Times: Tue-Thurs 4pm-6pm, Fri-Sun 12pm-6pm; www.ligca.org; Tube: Finchley
Road.

Museum of Domestic Architecture & Design 1850–1950 N11

Cat Hill, Barnet, Herts   (020) 8362 5244

The core of the six collections here is the Silver Studio, which was one of the leading independent design studios from the 1880s until the 1960s. This collection includes wallpaper and textile designs. Also of note: the library of Sir J M Richards (one of the most important figures in c20 British architectural history and a leading member of the Modern Movement in Britain); the Peggy Angus Archive; the Sir Charles Hasler Collection; the Crown Wallpaper Archive and the British and Domestic Design Collection 1850-1950. / Times: Tue-Sat 10am (Sun 2pm)-5pm; www.moda.mdx.ac.uk; Tube: Oakwood and then shuttlebus (runs every 20 mins) to museum, Cockfosters; Café.

National Sound Archive NW1

British Library, 96 Euston Rd   (020) 7412 7440   4–3C

This is one of the largest sound archives in the world. The reception area has a touch-screen introduction to the facilities, and you can listen to examples of the material held. You can also pick up free leaflets and a newsletter. There is a library and information service, which includes catalogues of the holdings (both here and, for example, at the BBC) and historical information on recordings. A listening service is also available, by appointment only. The catalogue is available on the website. / Times: Library and listening service Mon 10am-8pm, Tues-Sat 9.30am-8pm, Fri and Sat 9.30-5pm; www.bl.uk/nsa; Tube: King's Cross, Euston; Café, Restaurant.

Old Speech Room Gallery, Harrow School, Middx

The Old Schools Building, Church Hill, Harrow-on-the-Hill (020) 8872 8205, (020) 8872 8000

The Old Speech Room was built in 1819-21 as a place in which to encourage public speaking. In 1976, it was converted into a gallery to exhibit the treasures this famous school has accumulated over the years. There is a nucleus of antiquities, plus a series of temporary themed exhibitions which draw on highlights of the collection, such as c19 English watercolours, Modern British painting and some sculpture. For further information, including the dates of school holidays, visitors are advised to telephone. / Times: 2.30pm-5pm (closed Wed); closed school holidays; www.harrowschool.org.uk; Tube: Harrow-on-the-Hill (then 258 bus).

Shri Swaminarayan Mandir NW10

105-119 Brentfield Rd   (020) 8965 2651   1–1A

The largest outside India (according to the Guinness Book of World Records), this intriguing Hindu temple is a peculiar addition to the skyline of the north-west London suburbs. It was inspired by the c18 guru, Lord Swaminarayan, who walked the length of India preaching the values of social care. The temple was built with the use of 2000 tons of Italian marble and nearly 3000 tons of Bulgarian limestone, which was all shipped to India to be shaped by more than 1000 skilled craftsmen before being brought to Neasden for assembly, thus being constructed by traditional means. For a small fee, visitors can see an exhibition about Hinduism and watch a 12-minute video show explaining how and why the Mandir (place of worship) was constructed. / Times: 9am-6pm; www.swaminarayan .org; Tube: Neasden.

Stables Art Centre & Gallery NW2

Dollis Hill Ln (Gladstone Park)   (020) 8452 8655   1–1A

A contemporary art gallery, housed in the former stables of Dollis Hill House, exhibiting works by local and national artists. / Times: Thu-Sun 11am-6pm (Sept.-March 5pm); Tube: Dollis Hill or Neasden.

Stephens Collection N3

Avenue House, 15-17 East End Rd   (020) 8346 7812

In 1918, Henry Charles 'Inky' Stephens bequeathed Avenue House and its grounds to the public. (Stephens Senior was the inventor of the famous blue-black writing fluid that writes blue and dries black, and which because of its indelible nature is still used for signing marriage registers.) Since 1993, Avenue House has housed a collection of artefacts relating to ink and ink products, including original enamel signs, quill and steel-nibbed pens. / Times: Tue-Thu 2pm-4.30pm & by appt; www.avenuehouse.org.uk; Tube: Finchley Central; Picnic area.

Two10 Gallery NW1

210 Euston Rd   (020) 7611 8888   4–4C

Part of the Wellcome Trust (see also), this science-based art gallery presents about three temporary exhibitions a year. The media vary but the focus is always on exploring the relationship between medical science and art. A past exhibition, 'Shelf Life' peered into our medicine cabinets in a move to clarify myths about our home healthcare. / Times: Mon-Fri 9am-6pm; www.wellcome.ac.uk; Tube: Euston, Euston Square.

Wellcome Trust NW1
183 Euston Rd   (020) 7611 8888   4–4C
The trust houses two relatively small exhibitions: the Library Reading Room has a small, but regularly changing, exhibition on the history of medicine; and the Modern Medicine Reading Room exhibits post-1850 objects and printed ephemera from the archives, with themes such as temperance and veterinary medicines (including an up-to-date medical database). Those interested in the medical theme should combine this visit with a trip to the Two10 Gallery (see also) just across the road.
/ Times: Mon-Fri 9am-5pm, Sat 9am-1pm (Information Service); Mon, Wed & Fri 9.45am-5.15pm (Tue & Thu 7.15pm), Sat 9.45am-1pm (History of Medicine Gallery); www.wellcome.ac.uk; Tube: Euston, Euston Square.

The York Gate Collections NW1
Marylebone Rd   (020) 7873 7318   2–1A
A newly-opened museum showcasing the academy's collection of every variety of fine instrument, manuscripts and memorabilia. The star attraction is the selection of stringed instruments by the greatest Italian makers (most famously from the workshop of Stradivarius), and – coming soon – a whole floor dedicated to English pianos. You can watch instruments being worked on in the academy's maintenance shop and hear regular demonstrations of instruments in the collection. (See also Royal Academy of Music, page 39.) / Times: Mon-Fri 12.30pm-6pm, Sat & Sun 2pm-5.30pm; www.ram.ac.uk/museum; : Baker Street.

Outdoor attractions

Abney Park Cemetery N16
Stoke Newington High St   (020) 7275 7557   1–1C
A surprisingly countrified place (originally laid out as an arboretum), this cemetery that doubles as a nature reserve took over (around 1840) from Bunhill Fields as the final resting place of London's dissenters and non-conformists. General Booth, founder of the Salvation Army, is among those interred here, along with James Braidwood, first Superintendent of the London Fire Engine Establishment. The main entrance has been restored and there is a visitor centre which has information boards covering the geology of the stones of the site, its history and the (mainly local) characters buried here. Throughout the year there are various nature-related events, for which pamphlets can be obtained at the visitor centre, by phone or from the website . / Times: summer 9am-7pm, winter 9am-3pm; visitor centre, generally 10am-7pm; www.abney-park.org.uk; BR: Stoke Newington.

Alexandra Palace N22
Alexandra Palace Way   (020) 8365 2121
This 200-acre north London park is made rather special by its panoramic views over the metropolis as well as its historical associations as the site of the world's first television broadcast in 1936. The popular Grove Shows have been running for a decade – live music every Sunday afternoon between June and August and, during school holidays, high-quality performances for kids. Permanent attractions include a children's playground, an animal enclosure (with donkeys and deer) and a conservation area (near the Wood Green entrance). / Times: 24 hours; www.alexandrapalace.com; Tube: Wood Green (then W3 bus or free shuttle service that is available most days).

Camden Lock NW1
Chalk Farm Rd   (020) 7284 2084   4–2B
The slightly more upmarket side of Camden Market, with fashions, jewellery, books and crafts among the enormous variety of items on display. The lock is open all week, but, as with the rest of the market, Sat and Sun are the peak times for a visit. There are frequent summer attractions (generally during the week), such as street theatre, music and art shows – phone for details. / Times: 10am-6pm; www.camdenlockmarket.com; Tube: Camden Town, Chalk Farm; Café, Restaurant.

Camden Market NW1
Camden High St (and surrounding area)   4–2B
At the weekend, the whole of hip young London seems to descend on Camden for its vibrant markets – together with the tourists, they make it one of the most visited attractions in town. (In fact, the Underground stations are closed for much of the day due to overcrowding, so be prepared to walk, or know the bus routes!) By no means are prices particularly bargain basement though, and unless you are shopping for the latest style, the real point of the trip is to stroll around window-shopping, people-watching and listening to the omnipresent musical beats. As with all crowded markets, keep a close eye on your belongings. / Times: Thu-Sun 9am-5pm; www.camdenlock.net/cammarket; Tube: Camden Town, Chalk Farm.

Camley Street Natural Park NW1
12 Camley St   (020) 7833 2311   4–3C
In the heart of King's Cross – on Regent's Canal (though not accessible from it) – this community nature reserve is also a designated Local Nature Reserve. The variety of wildlife habitats include a marsh, a pond and a wood. Run by the London Wildlife Trust, it is one of the more than 50 nature reserves, of varying sizes, within the London area. There are some free events here during the year, for example the Spring Fun Days, Frog Day and the Camley Street Apple Day in October. There is an ongoing educational programme and a variety of children's events take place year-round – call for details. Donations are appreciated. / Times: Mon-Thu 9am-5pm (or dusk, if first), Sat & Sun in summer 11am-5pm, in winter 10am-4pm; www.wildlondon.org.uk; Tube: King's Cross; Picnic area.

Chapel Market N1
Liverpool Rd   (020) 7289 4371   4–3D
This diverse street market on the fringes of Islington is most popular at weekends and sells fruit, vegetables, fish, flowers and plants as well as a limited variety of general goods including fabrics and clothing. / Times: Tue-Sun 9am-6pm; Tube, Bus: Angel.

Coldfall Wood N10
Creighton Av   (020) 8348 6005
These 35 acres of ancient woodland to the north of Muswell Hill are of great ecological interest, and demonstrate examples of the returning fashion for traditional coppice management. If you intend to explore, call the Conservation Office who can provide you with further information, and the leaflet, Historic Woodlands in Haringey. / Tube: East Finchley.

Finsbury Park* N4
Seven Sisters Rd   (020) 8802 2612   4–1D
A large part of the 115 acres of this Victorian park is taken up with various sports facilities and a boating lake, so there's often a lot of activity. (You can even go fishing – but there's a charge for a licence.) There are several playgrounds, and a variety of small-scale children's events throughout the year, such as Easter egg hunts and fireworks night. (For more information about these, ring the Finsbury Park Action Group on the number given.) / Times: dawn-dusk; Tube: Finsbury Park; Café.

Freightliners Farm* N7
Sheringham Rd   (020) 7609 0467   4–2D
This three-and-a-half acre city farm in Islington is among the oldest in London. Amongst the usual farm animals are some rare breeds, and attractions also include an ornamental garden. There are many different activities: from sessions for under-4's to carpentry, horticulture, permaculture, animal husbandry, and straw-bale building. There's an 'Open Day' on the second bank holiday in May, where the attractions include sheepdog trials, sheep-shearing demonstrations, country crafts and children's activities. / Times: Winter & Autumn Tue-Sun 10am - 4pm, Spring and Summer 10am-4.45pm; www.freightlinersfarm.org.uk; Tube: Highbury & Islington, Holloway Road; Café, Restaurant, Picnic area.

Fryent Country Park NW9
Fryent Way, Kingsbury   1–1A
For those in search of real country in town, these 260 acres of unspoilt rural farmland, sandwiched between Wembley and Kingsbury, are pretty much the perfect answer. Nature walks, ponds and a wildlife area are among the attractions. / Times: 24 hours; Tube: Kingsbury, Wembley Park.

Gladstone Park NW10
Dollis Hill Ln   1–1A
William Gladstone was a frequent visitor to the fine Dollis Hill House (1824) which forms the centrepiece of this very varied 100-acre park between Neasden and Willesden. Other attractions include an arboretum filled with hundreds of exotic trees from all over the world, a pond with ducks and geese, and an old walled garden. / Times: 8am-dusk; Tube: Neasden, Dollis Hill.

Golders Green Crematorium NW11
Hoop Ln   (020) 8455 2374   1–1B
For the casual observer, spring is the time to visit this fine crematorium, set in 12 acres of landscaped grounds. At that time of the year, the front lawns are covered with upwards of 100,000 crocuses. Founded in 1902, the building features unusual northern Italianate architecture (by Sir Ernest George, RA, who also designed Claridge's Hotel). Those who have been cremated here include Marc Bolan, Gustave Holst, Charles Rennie Mackintosh, Sigmund Freud, Ronnie Scott, Peter Cook and Anna Pavlova. / Times: 9am-6pm (winter 4pm); Tube: Golders Green; Café.

Golders Hill Park NW11
West Heath Rd   (020) 8455 5183   1–1B
A pretty, landscaped park whose main attraction is a small zoo. Although, not exactly exotic, there are deer, wallabies, goats and sheep which can be fed. There are also a duck pond, woods and tennis courts. / Times: 7.30am-dusk; Tube: Golders Green; Picnic area.

Hampstead & Highgate Ponds NW3
Hampstead Heath   (020) 7485 5757   4–1A
Hampstead Heath boasts over 20 ponds – and you can swim in three of them. During the season (from the first Saturday before the May bank holiday to the third Sunday in September) you can choose between the Hampstead Pond (mixed), the Highgate Pond (men) and the Kenwood Pond (women). Showers and changing areas are available. All ponds limit children to those aged eight and over, and to one per adult. Swimmers who do not appear to be 'competent' may be asked to leave. See also Parliament Hill Lido. / Times: summer, mixed 7am-7pm, single sex 7pm-9pm (or sunset if earlier); winter, call to check; Tube: Hampstead, Kentish Town (then 214 or C2 bus).

Hampstead Heath NW3

(020) 7485 4491   4–1A

Hampstead Heath's 791 acres, administered by the Corporation of London, offer everything from a fine c18 house complete with art collection with formal gardens – Kenwood (see also) – to heathland which is as close as you get to real countryside near central London. There are also tremendous vistas – the views of the metropolis from some parts of the heath are so fine they have special legal protection. Other attractions include the bathing pools (see Hampstead & Highgate Ponds), concerts at the bandstand on Golders and Parliament Hills, free talks and walks. For kids there is a playpark, and a programme of free entertainment including Punch & Judy, magicians and clowns. A full diary of events is available with an A5 SAE every March from The Parliament Hill Staff Yard, Highgate Road, London NW5 1PL. / Times: 24 hours; www.cityoflondon.gov.uk; Tube: Hampstead, Golders Green.

Highgate Wood N6

Muswell Hill Rd   (020) 8444 6129

The 70 acres of Highgate Wood were taken over by the Corporation of London as "an open space for ever" in 1886. There's a small playground and a sports ground, but the attraction is essentially what the name suggests – an ancient woodland, with diverse flora and fauna, all just a few yards from the Archway Road. If you're planning to spend more than an hour or so in the wood, collect or send for a copy of the attractively illustrated free booklet, 'Highgate Wood', which lists the flora, birds and butterflies which can be spotted there. This, a newsletter and other leaflets on woodpecker trails, bat conservation trusts and the local natural history are available from the information hut or with an A5 SAE from Corporation of London, Highgate Wood, Muswell Hill Road, London N10 3JN. You might also like to explore the neighbouring 48-acre Queen's Wood (across the Muswell Hill Road), which is relatively wild and boasts an equally impressive selection of wildlife. (Both areas are part of the Parkland Walk, see also.) The information centre organises free walks and talks on an occasional basis – see website for details. / Times: 7.30am-dusk; www.cityoflondon.gov.uk; Tube: Highgate.

Kentish Town City Farm NW5

1 Cressfield Close, Grafton Rd   (020) 7916 5421   4–2B

A working farm of some four acres, with many typical farm animals and a wide range of activities for children. Opened in 1972, it was the first of its kind to be established and has played an important role in the development of the City Farm movement. / Times: Tue-Sun 9am-5.30pm; www.aapi.co.uk/cityfarm; Tube: Chalk Farm, Kentish Town.

Parkland Walk (Railway Fields Nature Park)
(020) 8348 6005

*Walking down a railway track might seem a rather hazardous
activity, but the redundant line between Finsbury Park station
and Alexandra Palace is actually a Local Nature Reserve and
offers an interesting alternative for a country walk in town.
The total length of the walk is four and a half miles and takes
around two hours. It is worth getting the free leaflet (which
includes a map, available from the Haringey Conservation
Officer on the number given) to avoid getting lost in Highgate
Wood, or giving up when confronted with the very unpark-like
Archway Road.* / Tube: Finsbury Park (south section), Highgate (middle),
Alexandra Palace; BR or W3 bus back to Finsbury Park (north).

Parliament Hill Lido* NW5
Highgate Rd   (020) 7485 5757   4–1B

*One of London's three remaining lidos, built in 1936, this
unheated, open-air pool is open from the first weekend in May
to mid-September but is free only for two hours every morning.*
/ Times: Mon-Sun 7am-9am; BR: Gospel Oak.

Primrose Hill NW3
(020) 7486 7905   4–3B

*The hill – the 206-ft high continuation of Regent's Park to the
north – is by far the most central natural vantage point over
London, and is therefore justly celebrated for its views (and is
one of the six legally protected viewpoints in the capital). When
there's enough snow, it's an extremely atmospheric place to go
tobogganing. There has been an outdoor gymnasium on the
site since Victorian times and there are still fifteen types of
exercise equipment available for year-round use. To get you in
the mood, the walk along the towpath of the Regent's Canal
from Camden Lock or Little Venice is a nice way of
approaching the hill.* / Times: dawn-dusk; Tube: Chalk Farm, Camden
Town.

Queen's Park NW6
Kingswood Av   (020) 8969 5661   1–2B

*A 30-acre Kilburn park owned and run by the Corporation of
London since 1886. It's not particularly large, but popular in
this relatively under-provided part of town, and especially good
for children, thanks to its large, supervised playground and its
paddling pool. There is also an ornamental garden and a fine
Victorian bandstand. The second Sunday in September sees
the annual Queen's Park Day – involving music, comedy, games
and a carnival – which draws big crowds. During school
holidays, the park offers childrens shows and storytelling
events.* / Times: 7am-dusk; www.cityoflondon.gov.uk; Tube: Queen's Park.

Railway Fields Nature Park N4

Opposite Haringey/Green Lanes Station   (020) 8348 6005
1–1C

This conservation park, in a former British Rail goods coal yard, has been developed for teaching primary school children about nature. There is a meadow, a woodland and a pond, and even a unique hybrid plant – the Haringey Knotweed. A visitor centre, with leaflets, provides information about the ecology of the site (as well as other places of environmental interest in the borough). / Times: Mon-Fri 10am-5pm (phone to confirm); Tube: Manor House.

Regent's Canal Towpath

Created as part of Nash's design for Regent's Park, these eight or so miles of the canal run from Paddington, along the north of the park, through Camden at Camden Lock, and on to the waterway's conclusion in Docklands in the east, where it joins the Thames at the Limehouse Basin. There is a towpath along its entire length which passes through tunnels and alongside locks, and past the perimeter of parts of London Zoo. The prettiest part is towards its western conclusion in the stretch through Little Venice W9. For the leaflet Explore London's Canals, send an SAE to British Waterways (London Canals), Toll House, Delamere Terrace London W2 6ND.
/ www.britishwaterways.co.uk; Tube: Camden Town (eastern end), Paddington (west), Warwick Avenue (Little Venice).

Regent's Park NW1

(020) 7486 7905   4–3B

Regent's Park's 297 acres have an atmosphere all of their own, perhaps because the park was in fact designed as a grand garden suburb. In the end, only eight of the 26 villas which John Nash planned at the beginning of the c19 were built (though a few more have subsequently been added). Queen Mary's Gardens have one of the finest selections of blooms in the country, including the Eudia, a very rare tree, and the lake boasts an impressive variety of wildfowl. The annual Music Village (early July) is Britain's longest-running 'festival of living traditions from around the world' and is a platform for international popular music, dance and crafts. During the summer, music is performed on a regular basis at the bandstand or at various other points around the park at weekends and some evenings during the week. There are also children's workshops during school holidays. / Times: 5am-30 mins before dusk; www.royalparks.gov.uk; Tube: Regent's Park, Baker Street, Camden Town, Great Portland Street; Café, Restaurant, Picnic area.

Roundwood Park NW10

Robson Av, Harlesden Rd   (020) 8838 1414   1–2A

A fine grade II listed 60-acre Victorian park in Willesden that has impressive floral displays and an aviary stocked with exotic birds. There is also a children's playground. / Times: 8am-dusk; www.brent.gov.uk/parks.nsf; Tube: Willesden Green; Café.

Waterlow Park N6
Islington   1–1C
Given to the public by Sir Sydney Waterlow in 1889, this 'garden for the gardenless' is situated on a steep hillside and has an unusual three-level lake, formal gardens and terraces. Lauderdale House (see also) is within the park. Facilities include a children's play area. / Times: 7.30am-dusk; Tube: Highgate.

Wembley Market HA9
Stadium Way   1–1A
Near what was Wembley Stadium, this is predominantly a clothing market with over 500 stalls. It is reputed as a good place for a bargain! / Times: Sun 9am-2pm; Wembley Park: Wembley Park.

South London

Introduction

South London boasts many of the best free destinations, especially for a family day out. Indeed, in **Tate Modern** the area boasts what is now the capital's second most popular attraction.

Just over Chelsea Bridge, **Battersea Park** is the only one of the central parks to benefit from a river frontage, and offers a wide range of attractions. A little further south, **Dulwich Park** is very fine (and, on Friday, can be combined with a visit to the **Dulwich Picture Gallery**). **Crystal Palace Park** is also an interesting destination (especially on a Sunday or a bank holiday afternoon, when the Museum is open).

To the south east – Greenwich – with **Greenwich Park**, the **Royal Naval College** and the **Old Royal Observatory** – makes an excellent destination for a day out (with the **Thames Barrier** not far away). To the south west, Richmond, and the great adjoining **Richmond Park** is also a very attractive place for a full day's exploration (especially bearing in mind the attractions around Twickenham, just on the other side of the river – see West).

If you're heading back to central London from some of the cultural attractions south of the river, such as the **Imperial War Museum**, it's worth bearing in mind that the early evening sees some of London's best free music, at the **National Theatre** and the **Royal Festival Hall** – posters on the South Bank list all the free events for the current month.

Croydon Tourist Information Centre, Surrey
Katharine St   (020) 8253 1009
/ Times: Mon-Fri 9am-6pm (Sat 5pm), Sun 2pm-5pm; www.croydononline.org; Tube: Southwark.

Greenwich Tourist Information Centre SE10
Pepys House, 2 Cutty Sark Gardens   (020) 8858 6376
/ Times: Mon-Sun 10am-5pm; www.greenwich.gov.uk; DLR: Cutty Sark.

Lewisham Tourist Information Centre SE13
199-201 Lewisham High St   (020) 8297 8317 .
/ Times: Mon 10am-5pm, Tue-Fri 9am-5pm, Sat 10am-4pm; www.lewisham.gov.uk; BR: Lewisham, Ladywell.

Richmond Tourist Information Centre, Surrey
The Old Town Hall, Whittaker Av, Richmond
(020) 8940 9125
/ Times: Mon-Sat 10am-5pm, Sun (May-Sep) 10.30am-1.30pm; www.richmond.gov.uk; Tube: Richmond.

Riverside walks

Arguably the finest walking in London, and certainly some of its best vistas, can be enjoyed on the mostly continuous paths which run along the Thames, on both the north and south banks from Kingston in the west to Docklands in the east.

The south bank is, on balance, the better place to walk, because it is generally more peaceful and it gives views of the almost invariably more picturesque north bank. (If you get bored, the distances between bridges are generally quite short so you can always swap sides.)

The most rural-feeling of the more central stretches of the river is the (often muddy) towpath on the south bank between Putney Bridge and Barnes Bridge. A good route to try begins at the half-way point, at Hammersmith Bridge – walk down to Barnes Bridge and circle back on the north bank (which is also attractive in this area). There are many good pubs at Hammersmith, some with a river view, so you might like to time your return to coincide with lunch.

If it's a walk in the centre of town you're after, there is a fine continuous stretch between the Houses of Parliament and Tower Bridge, along Victoria Embankment (the north bank of the river). In the City the walk leads you past the picturesque Tower of London to St Katharine's Dock (see also).

For another stroll on the same stretch of river, one of the nicest places, not least because it is away from the traffic, is along the south bank from Westminster Bridge – there are magnificent views (especially of the Houses of Parliament and St Paul's) and it is a particularly nice walk at sunset. Some of the best views in London is from the new twin footbridges either side of Hungerford railway bridge (between Embankment Tube and the South Bank Centre).

Heading east from County Hall and the impressive Millennium Wheel, you will pass the South Bank Centre and National Theatre. The second-hand bookstall under Waterloo Bridge is a great place to stop and browse. Beyond this is Gabriel's Wharf – with attractive gardens and a shopping area, it is particularly busy on a sunny day – and the ITV television studios. Continue east, past the Oxo Tower, which brings you to the area now known as 'Bankside' – Tate Modern and the impressive reconstruction of Shakespeare's Globe Theatre are features. End at the famous 'wobbly' Millennium footbridge, and the walk across the river to St Paul's provides a truly dramatic finale.

As you near London Bridge, the river path diverts inland, taking you along the atmospheric Clink Street, towards Southwark Cathedral and Borough Market – this area gets quite crowded at weekends. If you wander even further east, you will be able to see Tower Bridge in the distance, and will pass the new Greater London Authority building, designed by Norman Foster.

Other Thames-side walks to consider include a stroll along the riverside path in Battersea Park (see also), the north bank to the east of Kew Bridge, and, further out of town, the extremely pretty stretch at Richmond – there is quite a number of riverside pubs to distract you.

Indoor attractions

Addington Palace, Surrey
Gravel Hill, Croydon   (020) 8662 5000
The Palace – home in its day to six Archbishops of Canterbury – was built in 1776 for Barlow Tregothick, Lord Mayor of London. It is set in a 'Capability' Brown landscape and is of interest both for its architecture and its history. Parts of the Palace were restored in 1900 by Norman Shaw and the décor of the rooms dates from then. The Great Hall is lined with polished Italian walnut and the impressive fireplace is made from Italian marble. Now a conference and banqueting suite, the palace is open six days a year for free guided tours – call or check the website for details. / Times: -free open days throughout year;[see below] sund or mon 2.00pm -4.30pm; www.addington-palace.co.uk; BR: East Croydon (then 466 bus or no.3 tram); Café.

Age Exchange Reminiscence Centre SE3
11 Blackheath Village   (020) 8318 9105   1–4D
The highlight here is the charming '30s general shop with its genuine fittings and original stock. This "hands-on museum of the 1930s and 1940s" should interest anyone who can remember those days, as well as those who cannot. There is a changing temporary exhibition at the rear. The café serves tea and cakes in period style – in the garden in fine weather. For large groups visiting, a donation is asked for. / Times: mon-sat 10-5; www.age-exchange.org.uk; BR: Blackheath; Café.

The Bargehouse SE1
Oxo Tower Wharf, Bargehouse St   (020) 740 12255
5–3A
*A wander around the design shops of Oxo Tower combines well
with a visit to the Bargehouse (admission to the gallery is free
but some exhibitions may charge). Contemporary international
artists from all disciplines are represented, and the exhibitions
change every three weeks (see also the riverside walk).*
/ Times: 11.00am-6.00pm 7 days; www. oxotower.co.uk; Tube: Blackfriars,
Southwark, Waterloo; Café, Restaurant.

Beaconsfield Contemporary Art SE11
22 Newport St   (020) 7582 6465   1–3C
*Most exhibitions are free at this contemporary gallery located
in the former Lambeth Ragged School in Vauxhall. The gallery
sponsors solo installations by artists as well as group shows,
sometimes in collaboration with other international
organisations.* / Times: hours vary by exhibition, call to check (generally
Weds-Sun or Thurs Sun); www.beaconsfield.ltd.uk; Tube: Vauxhall, Lambeth
North, Waterloo.

Bethlem Royal Hospital Archives & Museum, Kent
Monks Orchard Rd, Beckenham   (020) 8776 4227
*Founded in 1247, Bethlem Royal Hospital, was home to many
paintings and drawings by artists who have suffered mental
disorder some of whom were incarcerated there. These include
works by artist Richard Dadd (1817-1886), who spent 42
years in criminal lunatic asylums, the dancer Nijinsky, and one
Jonathan Martin whose prophetic dreams led him to set fire to
York Minster in 1829. In addition, the museum has some
material relating to the history of Bethlem.* / Times: museum
Mon-Fri 9.30am-5pm, but best to check in advance; archives by appointment;
www.bethlemheritage.org.uk; BR: Eden Park, or East Croydon (then 119, 194,
or 198 bus); Café.

Bexley Heritage Trust, Kent
Hall Place, Bourne Rd, Bexley   (01322) 526574
*Formerly known as Bexley Museum, the building is part Tudor
and part Jacobean and is set in extensive gardens and
nurseries on the bank of River Cray. The museum contains
displays of local geology, natural history and archaeology, plus a
mock-up of a Victorian bath! There are varied temporary
exhibitions, mostly on a local history theme, and modern arts
and crafts displays.* / Times: Mon-Sat 10am-5pm (winter 4.15pm), Sunday
2pm-6pm (summer); www.hallplaceandgardens.com; BR: Bexley, Bexley Heath;
Café.

Black Cultural Archives SW9
378 Coldharbour Ln (020) 7738 4591 1–4C
*Every aspect of the history of black people in Britain is covered
by the collections of this Brixton museum (in conjunction with
Middlesex University). There are also changing exhibitions and
displays of work by black artists. Black people have been a
permanent part of the population for over 400 years, but no
comprehensive museum yet exists to chart their history:
National Lottery funding has been secured to develop these
archives and a new site into a larger national museum of black
history and culture.* / Times: Mon-Fri 1pm-4pm, Sat by appointment only;
www.aambh.org.uk; Tube: Brixton.

Blewcoat School SW1
23 Caxton St (020) 7222 2877 2–4C
*In 1709, local brewer William Green paid for the building of
this single room. Its aim was to provide an education for poor
children, and it was indeed used as a school until 1926. Bought
by the National Trust in 1954, restored in 1975, it is now the
Trust's London Gift Shop and Information Centre.* / Times: Mon-Fri
10am-5.30pm; www.nationaltrust.org.uk; Tube: St James's Park.

Borough Market SE1
8 Southwark St (020) 7407 1002 5–4C
*Since 1754 there's been a fruit and veg market at this south
bank location, occupying a hugely atmospheric Victorian
structure set into the railway arches near London Bridge
station. Rail planners perennially threaten to flatten it to
improve journey times. Prior to 1998, it was primarily of
interest to the wholesalers, who ply their trade from 10pm to
8am nightly. The last five years, though, has since the
establishment of a hugely popular "Fine Food Fair" which
operates on Friday and Saturday. Food producers from all over
the UK (and Europe) set up over 60 stalls, from which you can
'try and buy' goods from cheese to organic chocolate. The very
characterful surrounding area (especially Park Street) has also
been colonised by gourmet food shops, so foodies can now
window shop all week long. Southwark Festival's annual food
festival is also held here (see also).* / Times: Fri 12pm-6pm; Sat 9am -
4pm; www.boroughmarket.org.uk; Tube: London Bridge, Borough; Café,
Restaurant, Picnic area.

Bromley Museum, Kent

The Priory, Church Hill, Orpington   (01689) 873826
*This local history museum is housed in a largely medieval
building, set in attractive gardens. Exhibitions, which take place
in the Great Hall, include "archaeology of the borough till
Domesday", a social history gallery, the Archaeology Gallery
and a varied programme of temporary exhibitions, including
paintings and crafts by locals. One highlight is Bromley's first
fire engine which dates from the early c19, and another display
commemorating Sir John Lubbock, the first Lord Avebury
(1834-1913), whom we have to thank for bank holidays.
There are also a number of free family events throughout the
year – telephone for details. / Times: Apr-Oct 1pm (Sat 10am)-5pm;
Nov-Mar closed Sun & bank hols; www.bromley.gov.uk/museums;
BR: Orpington; Café.*

City Hall SE1

The Queen's Walk   (020) 7983 4000   5–4D
*The home of Mr Mayor and the GLA, this extraordinary
building was designed by Norman Foster and opened in 2002.
Part of it is open to the general public including the exhibition
space where one can view the Assembly Chamber. In addition
all the meetings of the Mayor's Advisory Cabinet, the London
Assembly and its committees including the Mayor's Question
Time are open to the public. There is a public information desk
in the Lower Ground floor (Mon-Fri 9.30am-5pm) which can
provide details. If you would like a short talk outlining the role
of the GLA, please contact the Public Liaison Unit, (020) 7983
4100. The building is also open some weekends (usually 2-3
times a month). Please call or check the website for details.
/ Times: Mon-Fri 8am-8pm; www.london.gov.uk; Tube: Tower Hill; Café.*

Crystal Palace Museum SE19

Anerley Hill   (020) 8676 0700
*The museum tells the story of the Crystal Palace, erected in
Hyde Park as a temporary structure for the Great Exhibition of
1851. The glass building attracted much interest and was
moved to Upper Norwood where it stood until it burned down
in 1936. The museum is housed in a brick-built part of the
original structure. Exhibits are mainly photographs, including
pictures of the fire, as well as some Victorian souvenirs. The
museum is set in 200 acres of parkland – see also Crystal
Palace Park. / Times: Sun & bank hols 11am-5pm; BR: Crystal Palace.*

Cuming Museum SE17

155-157 Walworth Rd   (020) 7701 1342   1–3C
*Southwark is one of the most historically interesting parts of
London. Its museum (just south of the Elephant & Castle) has
a rather unusual basis, being derived largely from the objects
collected by the Cuming family between 1786 and 1902.
There are five temporary exhibitions a year. Occasionally, there
are early evening talks, which may be on a wide range of
topics. Special hands-on activities for children, such as dressing
up and handling replicas, are held all year round. / Times: Tue-Sat
10am-5pm; www.london-se1.co.uk/attractions; Tube: Elephant & Castle; Café,
Restaurant, Picnic area.*

De Morgan Centre SW18
38 West Hill LIbrary, West Hill   (020) 8871 1144   1–4B
An extensive collection of the works of William and Evelyn de Morgan, together with archival material relating to themselves and their circle. He was part of the Arts & Crafts movement and – though best-known for his ceramic tiles – also painted, designed stained glass, and later wrote novels. She was a painter, whose style was heavily influence by fellow pre-Raphaelite, Edward Burne-Jones. / Times: Mon-Wed 12pm-6pm, Fri & Sat 10am-5pm; www.demorgan.org.uk; BR: Wandsworth.

Deen City Farm SW19
39 Windsor Ave, Merton Abbey   (020) 8543 5300
Animals at this five-acre city farm range from the expected to rare breeds, and there is also an expanding pure breed poultry programme. The emphasis is on seeing and touching, and there are also information boards, and on weekends, there are barn owl and reptile demonstrations. An upcoming project is the incorporation of a Sensory Garden, which will provide a number of impacts on visitors' senses through sight, smell, touch and hearing. Donations are appreciated. / Times: Tue-Sun 10am-4pm (5pm summer months); www.deencityfarm.co.uk; BR: Wimbledon (then 200 bus to Fips Bridge), Collingswood, South Wimbledon; Tramlink: Morden Road, Fips Bridge; Café.

Dulwich Picture Gallery* SE21
Gallery Rd   (020) 8693 5254   1–4C
This is the oldest public art gallery in the UK (1811) and was designed by Sir John Soane. It is almost as notable for its neo-classical design as for its important collection of old masters, which includes works by Rembrandt, Van Dyck, Murillo and Poussin. There is a particularly good selection of c17 Dutch art and also some of the greatest portraits by Gainsborough and Reynolds. Perhaps because its scale is not at all intimidating, this is one of the most enjoyable galleries to visit and the building has great atmosphere – in addition, the extension has provided all sorts of new visitor facilities. A curiosity at the gallery's centre is the mausoleum, which contains sarcophagi of the museum's founders. There are three critically acclaimed international loan exhibitions that take place here each year, in spring, summer and autumn (call for details). Combine a visit here with one to Dulwich Park or Belair Park (see also), opposite. / Times: Fri 10am-5pm; www.dulwichpicturegallery.org.uk; BR: North or West Dulwich; Café.

Erith Museum, Kent
Erith Library, Walnut Tree Rd, Erith   (01322) 336582
This small museum, on the first floor of Erith Library, features displays of local history. There is also an Edwardian kitchen and displays about the River Thames and local industries. / Times: Mon, Wed & Sat 2.15pm-5.15pm; www.erithmuseum.org.uk; BR: Erith.

George Inn SE1
77 Borough High St   (020) 7407 2056   5–4C
The only remaining galleried coaching inn in London is c17 in origin and was mentioned by Dickens in Little Dorritt. *It is still a public house (leased by the National Trust to Whitbread) so anyone can go and have a look at its interior. Parts are extremely characterful and include the tavern clock which dates back to 1745. There are Morris dancing displays in the courtyard in the summer, and at around 8pm on the first Mon of the month (not bank hols) a group plays traditional English music.* / Times: Mon-Sat 11am-11pm, Sun 12pm-10.30pm; www.georgeinn-southwark.co.uk; Tube: London Bridge.

Greenwich Borough Museum SE18
232 Plumstead High St   (020) 8855 3240
It's 'all change' at this local museum, which moves in the autumn of 2003 from the upper floor of Plumstead Library to new premises at Woolwich Arsenal (at which time the above contact details will all change). It's a little early to say to what extent its permanent collections will be re-jigged – previously it has focussed on local geology, archaeology, wildlife and local history, with fox and badger displays being particularly popular with younger visitors; similarly regarding its programme of children's activities in holidays and at weekends (as well as afternoon talks and lectures for adults). / Times: Mon 2pm-7pm; Tue & Thu-Sat 10am-1pm & 2pm-5pm; www.greenwich.gov.uk; BR: Plumstead.

Hall Place & Hall Place Gardens, Kent, Kent
Bourne Rd, Bexley   (01322) 526574
Hall Place, a Grade I listed country house, was built in 1540 for Sir John Champneis (a Lord Mayor of London), and extended in the c17. Almost all the rooms are open to the public, including the beautiful Great Hall. The building also houses Bexley Heritage Trust (see also – formerly known as Bexley Museum) and galleries with regularly changing exhibitions. The award-winning formal gardens are laid out on either side of the River Cray and feature a Tudor-style rose garden, a herb garden and a topiary display depicting chess pieces and twelve heraldic animals known as the 'Queen's Beasts'. / Times: Mon-Sat 10am-5pm (winter 4.15pm), Sun & bank holidays 11am-5pm (winter-not open on Mon); www.hallplaceandgardens.com; BR: Bexley Village.

South London

Honeywood Heritage Centre*, Surrey
Honeywood Walk, Carshalton   (020) 8770 4297
*Alas, this c17 house (with Victorian and Edwardian additions),
on the edge of the Carshalton Village ponds, is no longer
generally free to enter. However, there are at least three days
a year when access won't cost you anything. These include the
anniversary of the museum (usually the first Sunday in
December) and the Heritage Open Weekend (mid-September,
with free tours of the house and gardens). When you do get in
you'll find an exhibition setting out the history of the borough
(Sutton), including an audiovisual display. Many of the rooms
have been refurbished in period style. If you are interested in
the changing temporary exhibitions and events, ring for details.*
/ www.sutton.gov.uk/lfl/heritage/honeywood; BR: Carshalton; Café.

Horniman Museum SE23
100 London Rd   (020) 8699 1872   1–4D
*'Free Museum' is carved in stone at the entrance of this
fascinating Forest Hill museum (adjacent to delightful, very well
maintained gardens which boast a bandstand and lovely views
over London). A visit here has something for everyone. The
building grew out of the enthusiasms of Victorian tea magnate
Frederick Horniman, who in 1897 opened this Art Nouveau
gallery to house his collection. It is divided into three main
collections – natural history, music and world cultures
(ethnography) – and contains some 350,000 objects, as well
as an aquarium. There is also an education handling collection
which has over 3700 objects from all three collections. There
is a good programme of talks and workshops in the museum,
arts and crafts every Saturday for children and music in the
bandstand in the summer. The museum has undergone a
major refurbishment and extension in recent years.*
/ Times: 10.30am-5.30pm; www.horniman.ac.uk; BR: Forest Hill.

Imperial War Museum* SE1
Lambeth Rd   (020) 7416 5320,
recorded information (0900) 1600140   2–4D
*Despite its macho image – which the guns outside the
entrance do nothing to dispel – this venue puts on such a
variety of displays that every visitor will find something of
interest. The heart of the collection, of course, is the fine
collection of planes, tanks and every imaginable weapon of
war. Using interactive video technology, however, the museum
also stages some spectacular exhibits including reconstructions
such as the World War I Trench and WWII Blitz Experiences,
complete with sounds and smells. Much of the material goes
far beyond the 'hardware' of war, with some exhibits telling the
human side of the story. The VCGC (Victoria Cross, George
Cross) Gallery, for example, displays an array of medals and
relates the stories of the people who won them. There's also a
permanent Holocaust exhibition. The museum presents a fine
array of exhibitions geared towards children, some enlivened by
actors portraying soldiers and other historical characters. The
grounds in which the museum stands – Geraldine Mary
Harmsworth Park – are also home to the Tibetan Peace*

Garden (see also). / Times: 10am-6pm; www.iwm.org.uk; Tube: Lambeth North, Elephant & Castle; Café.

Jerwood Space SE1

171 Union St   (020) 7654 0171   5–4B
Originally a Victorian school building, this 2,600 sq-ft art gallery hosts a year-round exhibition programme of one-person and thematic group exhibitions. The gallery is made up of three interconnected spaces and an adjacent outdoor Sculpture Space, and is home to the esteemed Jerwood Painting Prize. / Times: Mon-Sat 10am-6pm, Sun 12pm-6pm; www.jerwoodspace.co.uk; Tube: London Bridge, Southwark; Café, Restaurant.

Kingston Museum, Surrey

Wheatfield Way, Kingston upon Thames
(020) 8546 5386
This purpose-built Edwardian museum (dating from 1902) houses three major exhibitions (as well as an art gallery for temporary shows). 'Ancient Origins' illustrates the borough's past from pre-history to Anglo-Saxon times. The newest permanent exhibition, 'Town of Kings', continues the story of Kingston upon Thames from the Saxon period to the present. The Eadweard Muybridge Gallery is named after the local Victorian pioneer of cinematography, who proved that trotting horses do have all four hooves off the ground at one time. Highlights of the displays include the original Zoopraxiscope and a panorama of San Francisco from 1878. / Times: Mon, Tue & Thu-Sat 10am-5pm (closed bank hols except May bank holiday); www.kingston.gov.uk/museum; BR: Kingston.

Little Holland House, Surrey

40 Beeches Ave, Carshalton   (020) 8770 4781
The Grade II listed interior is one of the attractions of this former home of artist, designer and craftsman Frank Dickinson (1874-1961). Wanting to create a house that would meet with the approval of his mentors, John Ruskin and William Morris, he designed and built the house and contents (in the Arts and Crafts style) himself. It took two years and was finished in 1904. Highlights include the painted frieze in the master bedroom, the carved timbers of the living room and the decorated fireplace surrounds. / Times: 1st Sun of month, bank hol Sun & Mon (except in Jan) 1.30pm-5.30pm; www.sutton.gov.uk; BR: Carshalton Beeches.

Livesey Museum SE15

682 Old Kent Rd   (020) 7639 5604   1–3D
Southwark's museum for children presents a lively and varied programme of 'hands-on' exhibitions – past displays have included working robots and optical illusions. Exhibitions are directed at the under-12s, but parents and other minders are free to take part. There is a picnic area. / Times: Tue-Sat 10am-5pm (last entry 4.30pm); www.liveseymuseum.org.uk; Tube: Elephant & Castle (then 53 or 172 bus).

London Glassblowing SE1

7 Leathermarket, Weston St   (020) 7403 2800   5–4C

The Glass Art Gallery at this well-established glass-blowing studio has three special glass-blowing exhibitions each year, as well as two exhibitions in other media. Additionally, you are welcome to watch the molten glass being blown and transformed into beautiful objects. If you so wish, you can, of course, purchase an example on the way out. There are three open weekends a year, in spring, summer and at Christmas – call for dates. / Times: Mon-Fri 10am-5pm; www.londonglassblowing.co.uk; Tube: London Bridge, Borough; Café.

Merton Heritage Centre, Surrey

The Canons, Madeira Rd, Mitcham   (020) 8640 9387

Located in a c17 mansion house in Mitcham, the centre tells the story of the borough of Merton and its people, past and present. There is a changing programme of exhibitions and special events – a past exhibition was entitled 'The Glories and the Dispossessed'. Displays usually include photographic material, artefacts, videos and a 'hands-on' section. / Times: tues-thurs 10.00am- 4.00pm fri-sat 10.00am -4.30pm sun 1.00pm - 4.00pm; Tube: Colliers Wood (then 200 or 152 bus), Morden (then 118 bus to Vestry Hall), Wimbledon (then 200 bus); Tramlink: Mitcham, Mitcham Junction; Café.

Mounted Police Museum, Surrey

Mounted Training Establishment, Imber Court,
East Molesey   (020) 8247 5480

Horses are trained here for public duty and ceremonies. To get to the museum you pass through the stables themselves – the small collection contains artefacts relating to the mounted branch since 1920, with paintings, documents, flags and regalia. / Times: by written appointment (groups & clubs preferred); BR: Thames Ditton.

Museum of Garden History SE1

Church of St Mary-at-Lambeth, Lambeth Palace Rd
(020) 7401 8865   2–4D

The world's first Museum of Garden History occupies the restored church of St Mary-at-Lambeth next to Lambeth Palace (the London residence of the Archbishop of Canterbury). The Tradescant Garden is a replica c17th knot garden (herbs planted in interlocking patterns). It commemorates the John Tradescants – a famous father-and-son team of gardeners and plant hunters – and is planted with plants popular in that period. The Tradescants lived in Lambeth, are buried in the churchyard at the Museum, and were gardeners to Robert Cecil, Lord Buckingham and Queen Henrietta Maria, wife of Charles I. Donations are welcome. / Times: Open daily 10.30am-5pm; www.museumgardenhistory.org; Tube: Lambeth North, Westminster.

Old Royal Naval College SE10

King William Walk   (020) 8269 4791   1–3D

*Wren's baroque Greenwich Hospital (for retired sailors)
became the Royal Naval College in 1873. The extraordinary
Painted Hall (whose entire interior is decorated with paintings
by Sir James Thornhill) should not be missed – the body of
Admiral Lord Nelson lay in state there in 1806. The attractive
c18 chapel (decorated by James 'Athenian' Stuart) is also
worth a visit. (Services are held every in the chapel every
Sunday at 11am, to which all are welcome.) The Greenwich
Gateway Visitors Centre, at the entrance to the College,
contains a series of exhibitions related to maritime Greenwich,
Tudor Greenwich and Roman Greenwich. / Times: Painted Hall &
Chapel Mon-Sun 10am-5pm, except Chapel Sun from 12.30pm. Visitor Centre
10am-5pm; www.greenwichfoundation.org.uk; DLR: Cutty Sark Gardens.*

Oxo Tower SE1

Bargehouse St   (020) 7401 2255   5–3A

*The free public viewing platform on the eighth floor of this
South Bank Art Deco tower offers excellent views, especially
across the river to the City and St Paul's. The building itself is
home to the retail studios of artisans such as jewellers, artists,
furniture makers and ceramicists, as well as the gallery@oxo,
which often has photographic exhibitions. The nearby Bernie
Spain Gardens is a good place for children to let off steam –
you could picnic here or on the benches on the Thames-side
promenade between here and the Royal Festival Hall.
/ Times: studios Tue-Sun 11am-6pm, the gallery@oxo Mon-Sun 11am-6pm;
www.oxotower.co.uk; Tube: Waterloo, Blackfriars, Southwark; Café.*

Photofusion SW9

17A Electric Ln   (020) 7738 5774   1–4C

*This Brixton gallery has bi-monthly-changing shows by leading
international photographers. / Times: Tue-Sat 10am-6pm (Wed 8pm);
www.photofusion.org; Tube: Brixton.*

Poverest Road Roman Bath-House & Anglo-Saxon Cemetery, Kent

Poverest Rd, Orpington
(01689) 873826 (Bromley Museum)

*If you want to get an idea of what it was like to bathe in the
early years of the first millennium, visit this ancient bath-house,
which probably served a small settlement or farm complex
between AD270 and AD400. There is a public viewing building
from which the excavations can be seen, including a hypocaust
(central heating system). This region's popularity survived the
departure of the Romans – pagan Anglo-Saxons buried their
dead to the north and east of the Roman ruins, around
AD450-AD550; men, women and children were buried with
their weapons, jewellery and pottery, which can also be viewed.
/ Times: by appt; www.bromley.gov.uk/museums; BR: St Mary Cray, Petts Wood.*

Public Record Office TW9

Ruskin Ave, Kew, Richmond   (020) 8876 3444   1–3A

This is the national archive of England and Wales – 96 miles of shelving holding records created or acquired by central government and the central courts of law from the c11 until the present day. All the public records previously held at the original Chancery Lane PRO, are now housed at Kew, and this is where you find, for example, the Domesday Book, Jane Austen's will and Guy Fawkes's confessions. There are also temporary exhibitions. An education and visitor centre was recently added. / Times: Mon-Sat 9am-5pm (Tues & Thu 7pm); closed bank hol weekends, public holidays & much of Dec; www.pro.gov.uk; BR: Kew Bridge; Tube: Kew Gardens.

Pumphouse Educational Museum SE16

Lavender Pond Nature Park, Lavender Rd
(020) 7231 2976   1–3D

This building, formerly housing docks machinery, is now home to the Rotherhithe Heritage Museum and is surrounded by a nature park. The museum traces the story of Rotherhithe and its people, as told by objects found on the foreshore of the Thames during 12 years beachcombing by local man, Ron Goode. Objects include coins, clay pipes and dockers' tools. Donations are encouraged. The Nature Park has trails through an orchard, herb gardens and past the 'minibeast city'. Reed beds fringe a pond which is frequented by herons, swans, tufted ducks and dragonflies. / Times: Mon-Fri 9.30am-3.30pm; Tube: Rotherhithe, Surrey Quays, Canada Water (from latter 2, take a 381 bus).

Puppet Centre Trust SW11

Battersea Arts Centre (BAC), Lavender Hill
(020) 7228 5335   1–4B

The Trust's fine collection of puppets dates from the c19 to the present (and some of them are available for hire). There are also rare photographs, slides, posters and memorabilia. A Library, containing videos as well as books, is open for research. There are family workshops on Saturday afternoons. / Times: Wed & Sat 2pm-6pm; www.puppetcentre.com/; BR: Clapham Junction; Café.

Royal British Legion Poppy Factory, Surrey

20 Petersham Rd, Richmond   (020) 8940 3305   1–4A

Each year around 34 million poppies are made here, as is the wreath the Queen lays at the Cenotaph on Remembrance Sunday. The factory was set up in 1922, originally in south east London, to help ex-members of the armed forces who are disabled but who can work to continue to be gainfully employed. Individuals and groups are welcome to join a tour around this working factory. / Times: by appointment, Mon-Thu 10am & 1.30pm (Fri tour am only); Tube: Richmond; Restaurant.

The Royal Festival Hall* SE1

South Bank   (020) 7921 0600 (switchboard),
(020) 7960 4242 (box office)   2–3D

*The view across the Thames from the upper terrace of the
RFH is one of the finest in London, especially as the sun goes
down. In addition, the concert hall at the centre of Europe's
largest cultural complex offers an extensive range of free foyer
events (all of which are set out in the centre's monthly
programme). There's live music on Wed-Sun, 12.30pm-2pm,
in addition to the regular Commuter Jazz, Fri 5.15pm-6.45pm.
During the summer, there is the Great Outdoors series of
events on the river terraces (and sometimes even on the roof!).*

*The annual three-week Ballroom Blitz is an opportunity to have
a go at almost any type of dancing. There are workshops
during the day while the events in the evening range from
ceilidhs to '70s disco dancing.*

*While you're visiting the centre, you can take in one of the ever-
changing art exhibitions in the neighbouring Festival Hall
Galleries, which are open all day and evening. The Hayward
Gallery sometimes stages free events. / Times: 10am-10.30pm;
www.rfh.org.uk; Tube: Embankment, Waterloo; Café.*

The Royal National Theatre* SE1

South Bank   (020) 7452 3400   2–3D

*Its uncompromising exterior may have taken a while to win
Londoners' affections, but the interior of Sir Denys Lasdun's
riverside building has always found favour with theatre-goers.
Even if you're not going to a show, you can still explore the
various levels of the intriguing layout and view one or more of
the several art exhibitions, which are open all day Mon-Sat.
Or take in the music – it might be early or contemporary,
classical, folk or jazz – before evening and matinee
performances on Saturdays. There's also a summer fiesta of
free outdoor theatre, music and entertainment called 'Watch
This Space'. / Times: Mon-Sat 10am-11pm; www.nationaltheatre.org.uk;
Tube: Embankment, Waterloo; Café, Restaurant, Picnic area.*

Shirley Windmill, Surrey

Upper Shirley Rd, Croydon   (020) 8654 0899

*This five-storey brick tower mill was built in 1859, and last
worked in 1892. It was restored in 1998, and retains skeleton
sails, its fantail and a Kentish cap. (Note that due to the
number and steepness of the stairs the mill is not suitable for
the very young or for those who are less than fit.) / Times: Jun-Oct
1st Sun in month, 1pm-5pm; BR: East Croydon (then 130 bus); Café.*

South London Art Gallery SE5
65 Peckham Rd   (020) 7703 6120   1–3D

This elegant Victorian gallery shares its site with the well-known Camberwell College of Arts. It presents a changing programme of innovative contemporary works by international artists, including a lot of 3D work, and performance art too. / Times: Tue, Wed & Fri 11am-6pm, Thu 11am-7pm, Sat & Sun 2pm-6pm; www.southlondongallery.org; BR: Peckham Rye, or 36 bus from Victoria, or 12,171 or P3 bus from Elephant & Castle.

Southwark Cathedral SE1
Montague Close   (020) 7367 6700   5–4C

In origin c13 (but with many later alterations), this fine building, just over London Bridge, is a hidden gem. Being rather overshadowed by the fame of the cathedrals on the other side of the river, it benefits from an absence of crowds. It is, in fact, the oldest Gothic church in London (and was apparently the inspiration for Westminster Abbey). Nor does it want for historical associations – the Bard's brother, Edmund Shakespeare, was buried here in 1607, and that same year saw the baptism of university founder John Harvard. At 1.10pm you may hear an organ recital (Mon) and an instrumental music recital (Tue). Renovations completed for the millennium added a visitor centre (for which there is a small charge), a refectory and external illuminations. (For information on the exhibitions and special events, ring (020) 7367 6722.) / Times: Mon-Sun 9am-6pm; www.dswark.org/cathedral; Tube: London Bridge; Café.

Tate Modern SE1
Bankside   (020) 7887 8000,
recorded information (020) 7887 8008   5–3B

This new national gallery houses one of the world's largest collections of modern art – over 4,000 paintings and 1,300 sculptures. The Tate collection dates from 1900 onwards and, instead of being presented chronologically, is shown in four themed groups: Nude/Action/Body, History/Memory/Society, Still Life/Object/Real Life and Landscape/Matter/Environment. The collection includes important works by Picasso, Matisse, Dalí, Rothko and Warhol as well as contemporary work by artists such as Susan Hiller, Dorothy Cross and Gilbert & George.

Bankside Power Station was transformed into Tate Modern by the Swiss architects Herzog & de Meuron. The Turbine Hall, running the length of the huge building, provides a dramatic and gaping entrance to the gallery. Sir Giles Gilbert Scott (who also famously designed the red telephone box) was the architect of the original building (completed in 1963 and decommissioned in 1981). The new two-storey glass roof at the top of the building allows stunning views of the city from the viewing gallery and café. The top of the chimney is illuminated by the 'Swiss Light'. / Times: 10am-6pm (Fri & Sat 10pm); www.tate.org.uk; Tube: Southwark, Blackfriars; Café, Restaurant.

Wandsworth Museum SW18
The Courthouse, 11 Garratt Ln   (020) 8871 7074   1–4B
This local history museum tells the story of Wandsworth from prehistoric times to the present day. There are year-round temporary exhibitions that change approximately every two months, and also worksheets, competitions and holiday activities for children. Highlights are the fossilized skull of a woolly rhino (found under Battersea Power Station), a reconstruction of a wartime shelter and a re-creation of a Victorian parlour. / Times: Tue-Sun 10am (Sun 2pm)-5pm; www.wandsworth.gov.uk/museum; BR: Wandsworth, East Putney (then 37 or 337 bus).

Wimbledon Society's Museum of Local History SW19
22 Ridgway   (020) 8296 9914   1–4B
This small, voluntarily-run museum depicts the history of Wimbledon from prehistory to the present day and includes archive material. Until recently, of course, Wimbledon was at a good remove from the metropolis, and its rural past is well illustrated by the collection of watercolours, photographs and prints. Highlights are scale models of local manor houses which no longer exist. / Times: Sat & Sun 2.30pm-5pm; www.wimbledonmuseum.org.uk; Tube: Wimbledon, Putney Bridge (then 93 bus).

Winchester Palace SE1
corner of Clink St & Storey St   5–4C
The c13 town house of the Bishops of Winchester was damaged by fire in 1814, but the remains of some of the walls of the Great Hall, with its unique rose window, still make an impressive ruin today.
/ www.compassarchaeology.co.uk/projects/medsou.htm; Tube: London Bridge.

Woodlands Art Gallery SE3
90 Mycenae Rd   (020) 8858 5847,
Library (020) 8858 4631
This Georgian house has a great artistic tradition. It was built for John Julius Angerstein (the 'father of the Lloyds insurance market'), whose extraordinary accumulation of paintings was, after his death, acquired by the government to form the basis of the National Gallery's collection. Woodlands now presents exhibitions of contemporary art (often by well-known local artists) which change every month. The building, situated in a pretty garden, which visitors are encouraged to enjoy, is shared with the local history library (closed Wed, Fri and Sun), through whose exhibits visitors are also welcome to browse. / Times: Mon, Tue & Thu 11am-5.30pm (Sat 5pm); Sun 2pm-5pm; www.wag.co.uk; BR: Westcombe Park.

Outdoor attractions

Battersea Park SW11
Albert Bridge Rd   (020) 8871 7530   3–4D
This 200-acre park is one of the most popular and most central family destinations, and rightly so as it's full of things to look at and do – events are publicised on noticeboards. The long river frontage (punctuated by the Peace Pagoda given to the people of London in 1985 by a Japanese Buddhist order) has lovely views across the river to Chelsea and the Royal Hospital. Other attractions include the Pump House art gallery, a herb garden, a deer enclosure and London's largest adventure playground for 5 to 16 year olds. Excellent literature is available from the Park Office (to the left of the Albert Bridge entrance), including 'Introducing Battersea Park' which has a map, and well-produced tree and nature trail brochures. There is also a small children's zoo (for which there is a charge). A major restoration of the riverside promenade, to the style of its Victorian heyday is underway, and due for completion in 2004/05. / Times: 8am-dusk; www.wandsworth.gov.uk; Tube: Sloane Square (then 19 or 137 bus); Café.

Beckenham Place Park BR3
Beckenham Hill Rd   (020) 8650 2292
Woodland and meadows with walking paths that form part of the 'Green Chain' (see also). There's also a kite-flying slope and sports facilities (golf course, putting green and tennis courts). / Times: dawn-dusk; www.beckenham.net/parks/place; BR: Ravensbourne, Beckenham Hill.

Belair Park SE21
Gallery Rd   (020) 7525 1050   1–4C
Neighbour to Dulwich Park, Belair Park, of 30 acres, is relatively little known, but worth looking at, having been laid out in the late c18 in the classic English landscape style. The park is also home to Belair House restaurant. You can combine a visit with a trip to the Dulwich Picture Gallery (see also) or the Horniman Museum (see also). / Times: 8am-dusk; www.southwark.gov.uk; BR: West Dulwich; Restaurant, Picnic area.

Bermondsey Antiques Market SE1
Bermondsey Sq   1–3C
If you arrive at dawn, you'll have missed the best bargains at London's largest antiques market (so take a torch and dress warmly). As the sun rises, the professionals depart and the trippers take over. / Times: Fri 5am (or earlier)-1pm; Tube: Night buses N53 (from Trafalgar Square), or later Borough or Elephant & Castle; Café.

Blackheath SE3
1–4D

*For centuries the heath was wild and a popular haunt for
highwaymen. Now, this large, flat expanse of grass separates
the pretty village of Blackheath from Greenwich Park. There
are a couple of ponds (one for boating), but generally its
attraction is as a big, open space for running about on. A visit
here would combine well with one to the Age Exchange
Reminiscence Centre (see also).* / BR: Blackheath.

Brixton Market SW9
Brixton Station Rd   1–4C

*The characterful warren of streets and alleys around Brixton
tube houses as exotic a market as you will find in London, with
food and fabrics from Africa and the Caribbean, as well as the
mundane items you expect to find anywhere.* / Times: Mon-Sat
8am-5.30pm (Wed 1pm); Tube: Brixton; Café.

Chumleigh Gardens SE5
Chumleigh St, Burgess Park   (020) 7525 1050   1–3C

*Tucked away, behind high walls in the bland expanses of
Burgess Park is a collection of erstwhile almshouses (from
1821) and a multi-cultural garden. The garden is divided into
areas: Afro-Caribbean, English, Islamic, Mediterranean and
Oriental, and all flora are labelled. There are also two ponds.
Owing to the water, and the poisonous or spiny nature of some
of the plants, kids should not be allowed to explore
unaccompanied.* / Times: 10am till dusk (winter 10am-5pm);
www.southwark.gov.uk; Tube: Elephant & Castle (then P3, 185, 176 or 40 bus);
BR:Denmark Hill (then 42 bus); Café, Picnic area.

Crystal Palace Park SE20
Sydenham   (020) 8778 7148

*The Crystal Palace was an enormous glasshouse which served
as a hall at the Great Exhibition of 1851 before being
dismantled and moved to Norwood, where it was consumed by
fire in 1936. There's a small museum about it (see also).
However, there is much more to this large and attractive park
than historical associations. The permanent free attractions
include a maze, a children's play area and a unique collection
of full-scale Victorian models of dinosaurs. Regular events
include the annual Victorian Day (usually the last weekend in
June). Over the May Day bank holiday there is also an annual
vintage car rally. During the Easter and summer school holidays
there are special events for kids, some of which are free. Year-
round you can follow the Tree Trail – details about this and
other events can be obtained from the Information Centre (at
the Penge entrance).* / Times: 7.30am-dusk, information centre 9am-5pm;
www.bromley.gov.uk; BR: Crystal Palace.

Cutty Sark* SE10

King William Walk   (020) 8858 3445   1–3D

This famous tea clipper, built in 1869 at Dunbarton, is the only one that remains in existence today. It has been in Greenwich since 1954 in a special dry dock. If you visit around lunchtime, you will hear the cannon that is fired on deck every day at 1pm. Unfortunately, there is a charge for visits to the interior. / www.cuttysark.org.uk; DLR: Cutty Sark, Greenwich; Café, Restaurant, Picnic area.

Danson Park DA6

Danson Rd, Welling   (020) 8304 2631

The park (grade II listed) was landscaped in the style of Capability Brown and features an ornamental seven-hectare lake. The park lends itself to a wide range of recreational activities, particularly on the lake. In the summer, boat races are a popular spectacle, and in July there is a festival and a series of outdoor concerts. The park surrounds the c18 Danson Mansion, which was designed by Sir Robert Taylor, architect of the first Bank of England. The Mansion is being renovated by English Heritage and is open to the public on special viewing days only. / Times: Mon-Fri 7.30am-dusk (Nov-Jan 4.30pm), Sat & Sun 9am; www.bexley.gov.uk; BR: Bexley Heath, Welling.

Dulwich Park SE21

College Rd   (020) 8693 5737   1–4C

A fine collection of trees is the particular attraction of this pretty 75-acre Victorian park. The rhododendrons and azaleas are a beautiful feature – for these May is the time to visit. The Park Ranger service organises walks (such as bat-spotting on summer evenings) and talks throughout the year, and produces a quarterly events programme. There is also rowing on the lake during the summer months. You can combine a visit with a trip to the Dulwich Picture Gallery (see also) or the Horniman Museum (see also). / Times: 8am-dusk; www.southwark.gov.uk; BR: North or West Dulwich; Café, Picnic area.

Foots Cray Meadows

Bexley   (020) 8303 7777

This rural area of woodland and open parkland (landscaped by Capability Brown) follows the course of the River Cray, and is home to an abundance of wildlife – bird-watchers often visit in hopes of seeing kingfishers. There is a bridle path and the remains of Foots Cray Place, a Palladian mansion built in 1756, but destroyed by fire in 1949. (The walled garden and stable block survived.) Five Archers Bridge, across the Cray, is also worth a look. / BR: Bexley Heath, Welling.

Green Chain Walk
(020) 8921 5028

The Green Chain Walk is a 40-mile network of fully signposted footpaths linking together nearly 300 parks and open spaces in SE London. Starting from three points on the River Thames, the footpaths are a twisting network threading their way through parks, commons and working farms ending at Crystal Palace Park. The network allows plenty of opportunities for choosing circular walks or following a linear route and using public transport to return to your start point. The Walk is signposted from 22 nearby railway stations and served by numerous bus routes. For maps of different possibilities for walks, visit the web site or pick up a free leaflet from local libraries and Tourist Information Centres. Otherwise a full colour guide is available, providing maps, walking instructions and points of interest to see along the way (send a cheque for £3.50, payable to Greenwich Council to Greenwich Council, SE London Green Chain, PO Box 22119, London SE18 6WY). / www.greenchain.com.

Greenwich Markets SE10
(020) 8293 3110   1–3D

If you enjoy nosing around market stalls, it's well worth making a special weekend journey to Greenwich, which has what is possibly the most comprehensive – as well as the most attractively situated – series of marketplaces in London. The individual markets are: the Antiques Market, Greenwich High Road; the Open Air food market; Village Market, Stockwell Street; and the Craft Market – the original market (1837), formerly a collection of fruit and veg stalls but now selling arts and crafts. The Open Air Food Market, located at the side of the National Westminster Bank, sells home-baked breads and hot foods. / Times: Sat & Sun 10am-5pm, summer sometimes Fri; www.greenwichmarket.net; BR: Greenwich; Café.

Greenwich Park SE10
Park Office, Charlton Way, Greenwich   (020) 8858 2608
1–3D

These 183 acres, enclosed in 1433, constitute the oldest of London's Royal Parks. It was popular with Henry VIII, who was born locally and who held jousting tournaments here every year. It is one of the best outdoor venues, still offering something to entertain all the family. There are red and fallow deer in the deer park (established here in the c15), flower gardens and a children's playground. Brass bands play at the bandstand on Sunday afternoons and evenings during the summer – picnicking by the audience is encouraged. In May and July, there are family events. There is also a free summer football school during school holidays (Charlton Football Club, tel 020 8850 2866). The view from the top of the hill by the Old Royal Observatory (see also) is quite something, and don't miss the Information Centre (at the St Mary's Gate entrance) which has rooms explaining the history and wildlife of the park. For a summer events brochure contact events@royalparks.gsi.gov.uk. / Times: dawn-dusk; www.royalparks.gov.uk; DLR: Cutty Sark, Greenwich; Café, Picnic area.

South London

Lesnes Abbey Woods, Kent
Abbey Rd, Belvedere   (020) 8312 9717
*Taking its name from the c12 abbey whose remains still stand,
this 200-acre wood, together with the adjoining Bostall Heath
and woods (160 acres), makes up one of the largest areas of
trees in south London. The spring sees a tremendous show of
wild daffodils, and then wood anemones and bluebells. A rather
unusual attraction is the natural fossil bed, in which the public
can search for shark and ray teeth, and shells. The woods are
quite hilly, and it's a good idea to take stout footwear. An
information centre has been added adjacent to the ruins, and
from here, you can pick up literature on self-guided trails.
/ www.bexley.gov.uk; BR: Abbey Wood.*

London Wildlife Trust Centre for Wildlife Gardening SE15
28 Marsden Rd   (020) 7252 9186   1–4D
*For those looking for special gardening secrets – making an
area attractive to butterflies or how to cover a wall in ivy – this
is the place to go. The centre offers assistance with all matters
of natural, wildlife gardening. For extensive help, workshops
take place regularly. / Times: Tue-Thu & Sun 10.30am-4.30pm;
www.wildlondon.org.uk; BR: East Dulwich, Peckham Rye.*

Morden Hall Park, Surrey
Morden Hall Rd   (020) 8545 6850
*This informal 125-acre park, owned by the National Trust, was
laid out around 1860 as a deer park. It is given additional
interest by a complex network of waterways coming off the
River Wandle (which was designed partly to be ornamental and
partly to power the snuff mills which still stand), as well as the
two-acre rose garden which boasts 2,000 rose bushes. You can
also visit the three craft workshops, and watch local artists and
artisans at work. / Times: dawn-6pm; craft workshops 10am-5pm, daily
except Tue; www.nationaltrust.org.uk/regions/southern/Morden.htm;
Tube: Morden; Café.*

New Covent Garden Market SW8
Nine Elms Ln   (020) 7720 2211   1–3C
*Since 1974, this famous market has traded on a large and
unlovely Vauxhall site which shows little sign of its origins in the
charming central Georgian landmark. With over 250
companies on site, it's one of the largest wholesale markets in
the UK. It's best known amongst the public as a place to buy
flowers, but you can also spectate on the substantial trade in
fruit and veg and catering supplies. / Times: Mon-Fri 3am-11am, Sat
4am-10am; www.cgma.gov.uk; Tube, BR, Bus: Vauxhall.*

Nunhead Cemetery SE15
Linden Rd   1–4D

The second-largest Victorian cemetery in London, Nunhead was first opened in 1840. It is no longer used for burials (except in the eco-friendly 'woodland burial' area.) Restoration in 2001 rescued 50 memorials as well as Thomas Littles' beautiful Anglican chapel. Part of the grounds (which boast impressive views over London) now form a nature reserve, supporting a diverse range of flora and fauna (16 species of butterfly have been found). Free tours of the cemetery are conducted on the last Sunday of each month (starting from the Linden Grove gates at 2.15pm), and there is also an annual open day in early summer.

On the first Sunday of every month, you can join in the cemetery's ongoing conservation – tea and biscuits are provided to volunteers (who must be a member of the Friends, which costs £2 a year). Activities might include pruning, pond building or inscription recording – see the website for more details. / Times: 8am-4pm daily (6pm Mar-Oct); www.fonc.org.uk; BR: .

Old Royal Observatory* SE10
Greenwich Park   (020) 8858 4422   1–3D

At the top of the hill in Greenwich Park, it's now free to enter the charming c17 Observatory (which has one of London's few surviving Wren interiors), where the 0 degrees longitude line can be seen (and which also continues outside). Many people consider that being photographed with one foot in the western hemisphere, and the other in the eastern, is an obligatory souvenir.

The Observatory is the spiritual home of the Greenwich Time Signal (though the actual electronic clocks are now kept elsewhere). A longer-established visual sign of time passing is the red ball on top of the Observatory, which descends its pole at 1pm every day – its original purpose was to enable seafarers to set their chronometers correctly, which was essential if they were to be able to locate themselves on long sea journeys.

The view from outside the Observatory is possibly the best in London and also summarises the history of London. Immediately ahead, you see the city's imperial past (the Royal Naval College), to the west sprawls the City and central London, and across the river looms the future, in the form of the burgeoning towers of Canary Wharf. / Times: dawn to dusk; www.rog.nmm.ac.uk; DLR: Greenwich.

Oxleas Woods SE18
Shooters Hill, Eltham   (020) 8319 4253
One of the capital's last remaining ancient woodlands (some 8,000 years old) was saved from the road-builder's bulldozer in the late-1980s. The wood supports over 33 different species of tree and shrub, including the rare wild service tree, the hornbeam and guelder rose. Fungi proliferate, with more than 200 species, including the 'storybook' toadstool, the poisonous fly agaric (red with white spots). Worth a glance is Sevendroog Castle, a folly that was built as a memorial to Sir William James Bart in the 1780s. The wood forms part of the Green Chain Walk (see also). There is parking within the woods, accessible from Shooters Hill (A207) and some of the other surrounding roads. / www.greenwich.gov.uk; BR: Falconwood; Café, Picnic area.

Richmond Park, Surrey
Holly Lodge, Richmond (office address)   (020) 8948 3209
1–4A
*This enormous park (2,500 acres) was created by Charles I by enclosing farmlands, and was used for hunting. Some remains of Richmond Palace – the gateway on the Green and the restored Wardrobe buildings – can still be seen. The park has changed little in the last 300 years, and still contains some 700 red and fallow deer. Because it has been disturbed very little, the park offers some rare natural habitats and has been declared a Site of Special Scientific Interest and, in 2000, a National Nature Reserve. The Isabella Plantation (towards the Kingston Gate) is noted for its fabulous collection of azaleas, and views from King Henry's Mound (which may have been a Bronze Age burial 'barrow') stretch as far as the City.
/ Times: pedestrians 24 hours; vehicles dawn-30 mins before dusk; www.royalparks.gov.uk; Tube: Richmond.*

Royal Arsenal SE18
Woolwich   1–3D
After centuries of being closed to the public and decades of decay, the Royal Arsenal is now subject to a £130 million regeneration project that will involve leisure, commercial and residential facilities. It started life in the c16 as an ordnance store set up by Henry VIII and became the birthplace of the Royal Regiment of Artillery. Their barracks, on Woolwich Common, boasts an impressive Georgian façade and overlook one of the largest parade grounds in Europe. There's a museum (for which there is a charge) and also the newly developed Royal Arsenal Gardens. / BR: Woolwich.

South London
=======
South London

Surrey Docks Farm SE16
Rotherhithe St   (020) 7231 1010   1–3D
This well-equipped city farm is in a slightly away-from-it-all and picturesque location, on the banks of the Thames opposite Canary Wharf. In addition to all the usual animals, attractions include an orchard, a blacksmith's forge, a nomadic Mongolian felt tent, a herb garden, vegetable gardens and beehives – it is possible in the autumn for kids to help collect the honey. Family visits are free but there is a charge for groups. / Times: Tue-Thu 10am-5pm; Tube: Rotherhithe; Café.

Sydenham Hill Wood Local Nature Reserve SE26
Crescent Wood Rd   (020) 8699 5698   1–4D
This preserve of rare and ancient woodlands, some more than 400 years old, faced imminent destruction before the London Wildlife Trust took control in 1982. The area covers over 50 acres and is home to some 200 species of wildflowers and trees, as well as over 50 species of birds and mammals. The preserve also includes relics of an impressive Victorian garden, a remnant of a c19 estate. / www.wildlondon.org.uk/; BR: Sydenham Hill.

Thames Barrier* SE10
1 Unity Way   (020) 8854 1373
The Thames Barrier is the largest movable anti-flooding protection device in the world – it was built in response to the ever-greater threat posed to low-lying central London by high tides (which have been rising at the rate of about 75cm a century). The barrier spans the 520m Woolwich Reach and consists of 10 separate, massive, movable steel gates. The most spectacular time to visit is during the annual all-day test (in September or October), when the entire barrier blocks the high tide, but it's an impressive sight at any time. (There are also monthly closures, but these happen as early in the morning as possible to minimise closure of the river.) There is a charge for the visitors centre, but not for access to the riverside walk or the children's play area. / Times: Mon-Fri 10am-5pm, Sat & Sun 10.30am-5.30pm; www.greenwichinfo.com/tourism/barrier.htm; BR: Charlton.

Thames Barrier Park E16
North Woolwich Rd
London's first new urban park for 70 years is rather a remarkable sight and has won a bevy of awards since its opening in late-2000. Features include a 3km trench, 5m deep, to provide a microclimate for plants, and a riverside promenade. / Times: dawn to dusk; Tube: Silver Town (DLR).

Tibetan Peace Garden SE1

St George's Rd   (020) 7930 6001 (Tibet Foundation)
2–4D

This charming garden, situated in a park shared by the Imperial War Museum (see also), was dedicated in 1999 by His Holiness the Dalai Lama. The centrepiece is the language pillar, containing a message of peace in four languages – Tibetan, English, Hindi and Chinese. The garden's design incorporates the fundamental Buddhist image, the Wheel of Dharma, and contains sculptures, a bronze cast and native Himalayan and Tibetan plants. / www.tibetanpeacegarden.com; Tube: Lambeth North, Elephant & Castle.

Vauxhall City Farm SE11

24 St Oswald's Place   (020) 7582 4204   1–3C

It may be less than an acre in size, but this tiny farm, run on a voluntary basis, boasts a full range of farm animals. Look out for rabbits, geese, ponies, donkeys and sheep. There is also an ecology garden and some allotments. / Times: Tue, Wed, Thu, Sat & Sun 10.30am-4pm; Tube: Vauxhall; Picnic area (sometimes, Sun 14.00-16.00).

Well Hall Pleasaunce SE9

Well Hall Rd, Eltham

A rose garden, a stream and a waterfall, as well as a moat and colourful flowerbeds are among the features of this unusual park, surrounding a c15 Tudor barn (now a restaurant). / www.greenwich.gov.uk.

Wimbledon Common SW19

(020) 8788 7655   1–4B

The common – as everybody knows, home to the Wombles, who keep it clear of rubbish – extends to nearly two square miles, some of which is quite rough countryside, and there are several ponds with much birdlife. It is the setting for one of London's few remaining windmills, which now houses a museum (Apr-Oct) about the history of this type of machinery, complete with working models, for which there is a charge, albeit a small one. A new addition is a wheelchair track, on the nature trail, that allows those on wheels to cover part of the common. This trail also includes sign posts bearing nature information / Times: pedestrians 24 hours; vehicles sunrise-sunset; www.wpcc.org.uk; Tube: Southfields, Wimbledon; Café, Picnic area.

Woolwich Foot Tunnel

North Woolwich Pier, New Ferry Approach
(020) 8854 8888 ext 5493 (to confirm lift times)

Another chance to walk under the Thames (see also Greenwich Foot Tunnel) which combines nicely with a trip over the river, on the Woolwich Free Ferry (see also). / Times: lift service, Mon-Sat 7am-6pm, Sun 9am-4.30pm; tunnel 24 hours unless there is major maintenance work; BR: north of the Thames, North Woolwich; south of the Thames, Woolwich Arsenal, Woolwich Dockyard, or 180 bus to Greenwich.

The City

Introduction

The tiny, but very wealthy Square Mile is often likened to a city-state. It has its own ways of doing things which have been arrived at over practically a millennium of running its own affairs, and its long history has left it rich in historic buildings and institutions. Its wealth and importance are symbolised by its medieval **Guildhall**, where great banquets for foreign heads of state are held, and by the great cathedral of St Paul's – other great sights include the **Tower of London**, **Tower Bridge** and the **Monument**.

Trading and, later, banking were the foundations of the City's wealth. Today more international banks gather together in the City than anywhere else. Almost all trading and banking business nowadays happens over the telephone, or sometimes electronically without any obvious human intervention at all. For the casual visitor, the **Bank of England Museum** provides the only insight into these sadly now rather closed worlds. If you want to see institutions at work, the barristers' **Inns of Court** are some of the most interesting, picturesque and immutable of all – and most are open to the public to a greater or lesser extent.

The City also has indoor attractions such as the **Mount Pleasant Sorting Office** and the **London Silver Vaults** – both of which should be of interest to older children and adults.

If planning a visit, it's a good idea to arrive in the late morning and begin by visiting the City Tourist Information Office – there is usually at least one free lunchtime concert in one of the City's fine churches (many designed by Wren).

City of London Information Centre EC4
St Paul's Churchyard (020) 7332 1456 5–2B
The City has a conveniently positioned general tourist information centre right by St Paul's. It has copies of City Events, an excellent guide to the musical and other events happening in the City during that month. / Times: 9.30am-5pm (Sat 9.30am-12.30pm, closed Sun during winter); www.cityoflondon.gov.uk; Tube: St Paul's.

Liverpool Street Station Tourist Information Centre EC2
5–2D
The office is in the approach to the Underground station.
/ Times: Mon-Sat 9am-6pm, Sun 9.30am-5pm; Tube: Liverpool Street.

Suggested walk

An afternoon walk through the City, leads one through 1,000 years of London history. Begin at Tower Bridge and the Tower of London. Move west along Tower Street, which becomes Eastcheap, until reaching Monument, to learn about the Great Fire of 1666. Next, an interesting stop would be the Bank of England Museum. Follow King William Street north and west until it meets Threadneedle Street. The Bank is ahead of you, and the entrance to the museum is on Bartholomew Lane, to your right. From the museum you have two options. One is to head south along Queen Victoria Street until reaching St. Peter's Hill. Descending the steps to the Thames brings you to the foot of the Millennium footbridge, which connects the City with the Tate Modern gallery at Southwark (see also). Alternatively, you can head west from the Bank of England along Cheapside to St Paul's Cathedral. From here, it's not far to the Barbican. If you time your walk correctly – concluding around 5.30pm – you'll be able to take in an early evening performance in the foyer of the concert halls.

Indoor attractions

Bank of England Museum EC2
Bartholomew Ln   (020) 7601 5545   5–2C
Housed within the forbidding building of the Bank itself, the museum is at the very centre of the City of London and traces the history of the Bank from its royal foundation in 1694 right up to the present. There are four DVD interactive videos which help bring the institution's activities to life, by telling the role of the bank today as well as the history of bank note design and production. The museum has gold bars and a copy of every design of bank note the Bank has ever issued. Curiosities include documents relating to George Washington (a former customer), Kenneth Grahame (a former Secretary of the Bank, as well as being the author of The Wind in the Willows) *and the original cartoon by James Gillray which famously satirised the Bank as the 'Old Lady of Threadneedle Street'. The neo-classical Bank Stock Office by Sir John Soane, recreated for the museum, makes a graceful centrepiece and is used for temporary exhibitions.* / Times: Mon-Fri 10am-5pm; also day of the Lord Mayor's Show (2nd Sat in Nov, see also); www.bankofengland.co.uk; Tube: Bank.

129

The City

Barbican* EC2

Silk St   (020) 7638 4141   5–1B

Love it or hate it, the City's sprawling, concrete arts and residential complex is undoubtedly impressive, with its vast concert hall, theatre, cinema and sweeping internal spaces – the biggest arts centre under a single roof anywhere in the world. There are FreeStage events in the foyer (anything from jazz to Irish folk music) most days between 5.30pm and 7.15pm (and also most Suns 12.30pm-2.30pm) – see the centre's programme for details – and there are often special themed events on bank holiday weekends. Free displays, often by local artists, take place in the library foyer, and there other exhibitions in the Concourse Gallery, Foyer Gallery, Craftspace and Jewellery Case. / Times: 8.30am (Sun 12pm)-11pm; library Mon-Sat 9.30am-5.30pm (Tue 7pm, Sat 12pm); Concourse Gallery Mon-Sun 10.30am (Sun 12pm)-7.30pm; bank hols 12pm-6pm; www.barbican.org.uk; Tube: Barbican, Moorgate; Café.

Chartered Insurance Institute EC2

20 Aldermanbury   (020) 7417 4425   5–2C

The Institute's very characterful building (near the Guildhall) houses displays illustrating the history of insurance through the ages. The main hallway (not generally accessible to the public) houses the world's largest collection of firemarks – the metal plaques which, in earlier times, indicated that a building was insured, and by whom. However, there is also a small museum that tells the history of insurance and houses an old fire engine. The building dates from the 1930s and, ironically, it was the only building in the area that wasn't bombed in the Blitz. It's a good idea to phone before you set out. / Times: Mon-Fri 9am-5pm, but phone first to check the areas are not under private hire; www.cii.co.uk; Tube: St Paul's, Moorgate.

The Clerks' Well EC1

14-16 Farringdon Ln   (020) 7527 7988   5–1A

The source that gave the surrounding area of Clerkenwell its name was subsequently filled in and built over. Rediscovered in 1924 the well chamber can still be visited – you can see an iron pump and plaque from 1800, some c16 refacing work and a later wall probably from the c17. Access is by key from the local library, see details below. Groups – 4 to 15 people – preferred. / Times: Mon, Tue & Thu, by appointment with the attendant from Finsbury Public Library, 245 St John Street, EC1, tel: (020) 7527 7988; Mon & Thu 9.30am-8pm, Tue & Sat 9.30am-5pm, Fri 9.30am-1pm; Tube: Farringdon, Angel, Barbican.

Clockmakers' Company Collection EC2

Guildhall Library, Aldermanbury   (020) 7332 1868   5–2C

The Clockmakers' Company may go back only to 1631, but its collection of clocks dates from the c14. This single-room horological museum (which has been extensively refurbished over the past few years) contains a glittering and fascinating selection of timepieces including curiosities, such as the first electric clock. There is also a large silver watch reputed to have belonged to Mary Queen of Scots, and the one worn by Edmund Hillary during his ascent of Everest in 1953. To hear the collection at its best, make sure you are there at noon. / Times: Mon-Fri 9.30am-4.45pm; www.clockmakers.org; Tube: St Paul's, Bank, Moorgate, Mansion House .

College of Arms EC4

Queen Victoria St   (020) 7248 2762   5–3B

The College, which traces its origins to the c13, is the body empowered by the sovereign to determine everything relating to the granting of new coats of arms and the right to bear arms which have been granted in the past. The main part of its building is c17, while the impressive wrought iron gates came from a country house and were given by an American benefactor. The Earl Marshal's Court Room is one of the finest, secular, period rooms in the City to which the public has access. / Times: Mon-Fri 10am-4pm; www.college-of-arms.gov.uk; Tube: Blackfriars, St Pauls.

Family Record Centre EC1

1 Myddelton St   (020) 8392 5300   5–1A

If you want to trace your family history, you can now find microfilms of census, probate wills and non-conformist registers (formerly at Chancery Lane) and Birth, Marriage and Death Registers (previously at St Catherine's House) on one site in Islington. Benefits of the move include larger-capacity reading rooms and bigger refreshment areas. To apply for certificates, you need a document such as a driving licence or cheque card with your signature on it, or if you are not British, your passport or national identity card. / Times: Mon, Wed & Fri 9am-5pm (Thu 7pm), Tue 10am-7pm, Sat 9.30am-5pm; closed bank hol weekends & public holidays; www.familyrecords.gov.uk/frc/default.htm; Tube: Angel, Farringdon.

Guildhall EC1

Gresham St   (020) 7606 3030   5–2C

The hall on this site has been the most important secular building in the City since the c11 – many important events and glittering state banquets take place here. Much of the present building (which is on a spectacular scale) dates from 1411, and, although fire and bomb damage have taken their toll, a fair amount of the original remains. The magnificent hall is usually open to casual visitors (ring to check), and pre-booked parties (10-50 people) may also visit the Old Library and the medieval crypt. / Times: May-Sep, Mon-Sun 10am-5pm; Oct-Apr, closed Sun; www.cityoflondon.gov.uk; Tube: St Paul's, Bank.

Guildhall Art Gallery EC1

Gresham St   (020) 7332 3700   5–2C

The gallery houses the Corporation of London's collection of art, now numbering some 4000 items, which was started in the c17th. Works range from portraits of monarchs to a good collection of Victorian pictures. Around 250 works of art are exhibited at any one time along with a programme of differently themed temporary exhibitions (ring or check website for details). The gallery also houses the Roman Amphitheatre which is beneath the art gallery and dates from the second-century AD. / Times: 3.30pm-5pm, Fri 10am-5pm; www.cityoflondon.gov.uk; Tube: St Paul's, Bank.

Guildhall Library EC2

Aldermanbury   (020) 7332 1868   5–2C

This elegant library specialises in the history of London. If this is an area which interests you, this is a delightful place to while away a couple of hours. Information not available on the shelves can normally be retrieved from the stores within 10 minutes. There is an area where visitors can consume packed lunches. Housed within the library you can visit the Guildhall Clock Museum where you will find a history of clock and watch making since the c16th. / Times: Mon-Sat 9.30am-5pm (restricted service Sat); www.cityoflondon.gov.uk; Tube: Moorgate, Bank, St Paul's.

Livery Halls EC1

The proud and ancient livery companies of the City – originally trade guilds, now a rather grand cross between a charity and a gentleman's club – boast a large number of halls, some of which are extremely grand and historic. Gaining access to most of them is difficult, but it is worth applying to the City Information Office early in each year for part of the small allocation of tickets which they receive every February. The companies participating in the scheme vary, but have recently included the Goldsmiths, the Tallow Chandlers, the Skinners, the Fishmongers, the Ironmongers and the Haberdashers. Groups of up to 30 can arrange an appointment to be shown around the magnificent Fishmongers' Hall at other times by contacting the archivist on (020) 7626 3531, ext 257. (Note that the hall is closed from the end of July to the end of September.) The Corporation of London website (www.cityoflondon.gov.uk) has links to all the major livery company websites.

London Metropolitan Archives EC1

40 Northampton Rd   (020) 7332 3820   4–4D

The name says it all. For anyone interested in the history of London (and Middlesex) – or wanting to research their Londoner forebears – this City-fringe establishment offers a fascinating glimpse at city life in past centuries. There are documents, books, maps and photographs – many on open access, but some available only upon request, the earliest documents dating from c13. / Times: Mon-Fri 9.30am-4.45pm (Tues & Thu 7.30pm), selected Saturdays 9.30am-4.45pm (please call or see website for dates); www.cityoflondon.gov.uk/lma; Tube: King's Cross, Farringdon, Angel.

London Silver Vaults WC2

Chancery House, Chancery Ln   (020) 7242 3844   2–2D
*This intriguing, subterranean shopping mall, with its 40 or so
silver dealers, claims to offer the largest collection of silverware
under one roof in the world. All the items are for sale, with
prices ranging from £5 to £500,000, but you're quite welcome
just to go and browse.* / Times: Mon-Fri 9am-5.30pm, Sat 9am-1pm;
Tube: Chancery Lane.

Museum & Library of The Order of St John, St John Ambulance* EC1

St John's Gate, St John's Ln   (020) 7324 4070   5–1A
*The ground floor of St John's Gate houses the historic
collections of the Order which include Maltese silver and
furniture, pharmacy jars, paintings, prints, drawings and arms
and armour. All items reflect the history and work of the
Knights Hospitaller from the time of the Crusades to the
present day St John Ambulance. Tours can be arranged which
take in the Museum but also the rest of St John's Gate (see
also).* / Times: Mon-Fri 10am-5pm, Sat (library by appointment, exhibition rms
10am-4pm); www.sja.org.uk/history; Tube: Farringdon; Café, Restaurant, Picnic
area.

Museum of London* EC2

London Wall   recorded information (020) 7600 0807
5–2B
*One of London's most interesting and best-presented museums
offers 14 galleries of permanent and temporary exhibitions
revealing the history of the capital from prehistoric times to the
present day. The ever-changing displays might cover anything
from photographs of football fans to displays about royal
fashion. Star exhibits include the spectacular gilded Lord
Mayor's coach (wheeled out once a year for the eponymous
Show – see also) and a genuine c18 prison cell complete with
prisoners' graffiti. There is also a 'London before London'
exhibition in the Pre-History gallery, which charts the history of
the area over the last ten million years and includes some
1000 objects. At lunchtimes there are occasional free lectures
and films.* / Times: Mon-Sat 10am-5.50pm; Sun noon-5.50pm;
www.museumoflondon.org.uk; Tube: Barbican, Bank, St Paul's, Moorgate; Café.

Museum of the Honorable Artillery Company EC1

Armoury House, City Rd
(020) 7382 1533, (020) 7382 1537   5–1C
*The Honorable Artillery Company was founded in 1537 by
Henry VIII from the existing Guild of St George. It was directed
to "attend to the better defence of the Realm" and encouraged
exercise in handling bows and handguns. The museum was set
up in 1987 to commemorate the Company's 450th
anniversary. Highlights include uniforms, Chinese porcelain with
the HAC coat of arms, and swords. Donations are appreciated.*
/ Times: apply in writing for a visit; www.cbus.co.uk; Tube: Moorgate, Liverpool
Street, Old Street.

Oak Room EC1
173 Rosebery Ave   (020) 7833 9527   4–3D
On four days a year (ring for details), and only by prior appointment, this c17th room, designed by Wren's protégé Grinling Gibbons, is open to the public. It was built originally as the boardroom (in modern parlance) of the New River Company (an important early scheme to bring clean water to the metropolis), and has been moved from its initial location. / Tube: Angel (or 19 or 38 buses).

Old Bailey EC4
Newgate St   (020) 7248 3277   5–2B
The Central Criminal Court, as it is more properly called, is the site of London's most notorious trials. All human life is there, and there's usually something intriguing, amusing or just plain bizarre to listen to. If you're only paying a brief visit, the most interesting thing to do is to catch the cross-examination of a witness by a bewigged barrister. There are two public gallery entrances: Warwick Passage, off Old Bailey, and Newgate Street. Children below the age of 14 are not allowed. / Times: Mon-Fri 10.30am-1pm, 2pm-4pm; Tube: St Paul's, Blackfriars.

Prince Henry's Room EC4
17 Fleet St   (020) 7936 2710   5–2A
In one of the few buildings in the City to survive the Great Fire, this small room retains its original panelling and plaster work. The naming of the building is honorific only (referring to the eldest son of James I) and it now houses a selection of memorabilia of diarist Samuel Pepys. The curators are enthusiasts for the great man and are pleased to share their knowledge. / Times: 11am-2pm, closed Sun & bank hol weekends; Tube: Temple.

Royal Mail Mount Pleasant Sorting Office EC1
Farringdon Rd   (020) 7239 2311   5–1A
If you've always wondered how the mail gets distributed, a visit here should answer your questions. There are organised tours which cover the sorting office and the mechanical sorting equipment. To arrange a visit, call to book – individuals are welcome, though you will have to confirm in writing two weeks before you go. Children under 12 are not admitted. (Note: a previous star attraction, the Mail Rail – the unstaffed underground railway which distributes post around the capital – is set to close as we go to press, though exactly when is still uncertain). / Times: Mon-Fri 3pm onwards by appt; Tube: Farringdon, King's Cross, Chancery Lane.

St Bartholomew's Hospital Museum* EC1

West Smithfield   (020) 7601 8152   5–2B

Original archives, artefacts and medical instruments, together with video and sound recordings, tell the story of this famous hospital from its foundation in 1123 to the present day. Of particular interest is the Charter signed by Henry VIII preventing the closure of the hospital during the Dissolution of the Monasteries and eight sound recordings of doctors and nurses recreating their daily lives from 1500-present. Kids might particularly like the amputation kits and bleeding bowls, and the wooden head used for practising trepanning (drilling through the scalp). / Times: Tue-Fri 10am-4pm; www.brlcf.org.uk; Tube: Barbican, St Paul's; Café, Restaurant, Picnic area.

St Etheldreda EC1

14 Ely Place   (020) 7405 1061   5–2A

Britain's oldest catholic church (1250s) is the only surviving building of the Bishop of Ely's London residence, Ely House (referred to in the writings of both Shakespeare and Dickens). It has some very good gothic architecture, as well as a good choir which can be enjoyed at Sunday services. / Times: 7.30am-7pm daily; Tube: .

St John Ambulance Exhibition EC1

St John's Gate, St John's Ln   (020) 7324 4070   5–1A

Within St John's Gate (see also), this contemporary exhibition, Time to Care, tells the story of the St John Ambulance Association (formed in 1887) which today operates in over 43 countries. The exhibition showcases stories of St John Ambulance work and includes multimedia interactive exhibits, film and oral history, as well as paintings and displays. / Times: Mon-Sat 10am-5pm (Sat 4pm); www.sja.org.uk/history; Tube: Farringdon.

St John's Gate EC1

St John's Ln   (020) 7324 4070   5–1A

Built in 1504, the Gate was the entrance to the Priory of the Knights Hospitaller and has also been variously: entrance to the office of the Master of the Revels (licensing Shakespeare's plays); a coffee house run by Hogarth's father; a club venue for Dickens, Cruikshank and other c19th notables; a tavern; and – last but not least – birthplace of St John Ambulance. Tours visit upstairs rooms in the Gate as well as the c14 Priory Church & Norman Crypt (one of the few remaining in London). / Times: Mon-Fri 10am-5pm (Sat 4pm) Tours: (donations requested) groups must book - Tues, Fri, Sat 11am & 2.30pm; www.sja.org.uk/history; Tube: Farringdon, Barbican.

Salvation Army International Heritage Centre EC4
101 Queen Victoria St   (020) 7332 0101   5–3A
(With the re-development of the Salvation Army's international HQ, the museum is – as we go to press – in store and closed except to visiting researchers until some time after the building re-opens in 2004.) Its purpose is to help you discover the history of the Salvation Army and why its founder, William Booth, devoted his life to the poor and homeless. A 50 minute recorded tour of the exhibition is available at no charge. Call for further information and to ascertain the status regarding re-opening. / Times: Mon-Fri 9.30am-3.30pm; www.salvationarmy.org; Tube: Mansion House, Black Friars.

Wesley's Chapel EC1
49 City Rd   (020) 7253 2262   5–1C
John Wesley, the father of Methodism, had his chapel and house built in 1778 to the designs of George Dance the Younger. You can visit the chapel and Wesley's tomb, which are part of this fine group of Georgian buildings on the northern fringe of the City. (Wesley's House and the Museum of Methodism can also be visited during the same hours, but for these there is a charge.) / Times: Mon-Sat 10am-4pm, Sun 12pm-2pm; www.wesleyschapel.org.uk; Tube: Old Street, Moorgate.

Outdoor attractions

Broadgate* EC2
(020) 7505 4000   5–2D
One summer (end May-beginning of Sep) lunchtime, when the weather is hot, why not visit the City's Broadgate development. Most weekdays between 12.30pm and 2pm, this Manhattan-style complex of offices, shops and restaurants puts on musical or other entertainments (usually at some point including an unusual exhibition, in the past it has been a display of Spanish dressage with Andalucian horses). Giant chess and draughts sets are provided, too. During the winter, you could spend an evening (dress warmly) watching teams compete at broomball on London's only permanent outdoor ice-rink – or try ice-skating for yourself (there is a charge). A monthly diary of events – Broadgate Live – is available from the Arena office (or you can call to be put on the mailing list). / www.broadgateevents.co.uk; Tube: Liverpool Street.

Inns of Court
(020) 7427 4800 (Middle Temple); (020) 7405 1393 (Lincoln's Inn); (020) 7458 7800 (Gray's Inn); (020) 7797 8177 (Inner Temple); (020) 7353 8559 (Temple Church) 5–2A
Lawyers have clustered around the City since the earliest times. Even today, every barrister practising in England and Wales must be a member of one of the four inns of court (the Middle and Inner Temples, Gray's and Lincoln's Inns). These bodies

are effectively medieval colleges, with their own dining halls, libraries, gardens and chapels. They are also landlords to the barristers' chambers (offices).

All of the inns give the public access to some part of their territories, which are peaceful, charming and often of considerable antiquity.

Starting in the Temple, don't miss Middle Temple Hall, a large Tudor hall with a magnificent double hammer-beam roof. This area is also rich in historical trivia – not only was Twelfth Night first performed in the hall here by the Bard's own company (1602), but the Wars of the Roses took their name from red and white blooms plucked from the garden behind. The hall at the neighbouring Inner Temple is not open to the public (although the gardens are, between noon-3pm daily), but the main sight there is the Temple Church, the only circular church in London and one of London's oldest buildings (c12).

Leaving the Temple, and progressing up Chancery Lane, you come first to Lincoln's Inn, with its fine, sweeping lawns, halls (one c15, one c19) and chapel (noon-2.30pm only), and then to Gray's Inn, whose chapel and walks (at lunchtime) are open to public view. Organised groups can see the inside of the rest of the building, including the medieval hall, by writing to the Under Treasurer, Honorable Society of Gray's Inn, Treasury Office, 8 South Square, London WC1R 5ET.

The grounds of all the inns are open on weekdays. Mid-morning and mid-afternoons of weekdays are generally the best times to gain access to the halls and chapels – if you are making a special trip, it may be wise to call to confirm access. / Times: Middle Temple Hall 10am-11.30am, 3pm–4pm; call for other times; all temples closed Sat & Sun; www.middletemple.org.uk, www.lincolnsinn.org.uk, www.graysinn.org.uk, www.innertemple.org.uk, www.templechurch.com; Tube: Temple, Chancery Lane.

Leadenhall Market EC3
Whittington Ave   5–2C
For an atmospheric City experience, there's little to rival a stroll around this quite small, but wonderfully atmospheric and impressive covered Victorian market (whose architect was Horace Jones, who also designed Tower Bridge and Smithfield Market). It stands in stark contrast to the new Lloyds building, which towers over it, while a sprinkling of stalls and shops selling fine wine, fish and game give some clue as to how local workers enjoy spending the fruits of their labours. / Times: Mon-Fri 7am-4pm; Tube: Bank, Monument.

Leather Lane Market EC1
Leather Ln   5–1A
A street market for over 300 years, and still one of the most atmospheric in London. It's also relatively untouched by the tourist hand despite being in the heart of Clerkenwell, with the crush of shoppers mainly company locals and workers on their lunchbreak from nearby offices. The range of goods on sale

covers the usual bases: from fruit and veg to plants, jewellery, clothes and household goods. / Times: Mon-Fri 10am-2.30pm; Tube: Chancery Lane.

The Monument* EC2
Monument St & Fish St Hill   5–3C
The Great Fire of 1666 swept away much of the medieval City. The burghers of the day commissioned Wren to memorialise the devastation and the Monument – still the highest free-standing stone column in the world – was the result. Its height (202 feet) is the same as its distance from the baker's shop in Pudding Lane where the fire started. The story is given in detail in the large notice at the base of the column. (You can climb to the top, but there's a small charge.) / Tube: Monument.

Riverside Walk
See the introduction of the South section for suggestions of interesting walks by the Thames.

Smithfield Market EC1
Smithfield   (020) 7248 3151   5–2A
There has been a meat market in Smithfield since the 1100's, though the current building – designed by the architect for Tower Bridge, Horace Jones – was built in 1868. It's an extremely atmospheric piece of design (in a characterful and increasingly trendy bit of town) and was recently repainted with the aim of recreating the original colours. To this day it is the largest meat market in London. Although the public are not allowed in every section due to health regulations, it's worth an early morning visit which can be followed by a pint and full breakfast at one of the nearby pubs, which have special dispensation to open early (7am). / Times: Mon-Fri 4am-10am; Tube, BR: .

Tower Bridge* SE1
(020) 7940 3985   5–4D
One of London's great symbols, the bridge was built between 1886 and 1894. Despite its appearance, it is, in fact, a thoroughly modern steel structure, but was clad in stone to harmonise with the Tower of London. The halves of the bridge (originally steam-powered, but now electrically operated) can still be raised to accommodate large vessels needing access to the Pool of London – ring the number given to find out when the bridge is next scheduled to be raised. There is a fascinating display inside the bridge which explains the workings of the original machinery, but there is a charge. / www.towerbridge.org.uk; Tube: Tower Hill.

Tower of London* EC3
West Gate, Tower of London   (020) 7709 0765   5–3D
The Tower of London is one of the most interesting and historic sites in London and unfortunately charges handsomely for entering its precincts or visiting the treasures within (which, of course, include the Crown Jewels). You can get a good perspective of the medieval building from the riverside walk, however (and see also Ceremony of the Keys). / www.tower-of-london.com; Tube: Tower Hill.

East London

Introduction

Centuries of being the poor relation among the areas of London has left east London ('the East End') with a very different range of amenities from any other area. It means, for example, that in the inner city there is only one park of any note, **Victoria Park**. However, if you are prepared to go as far as the end of the Central Line, you will, in **Epping Forest**, find the largest medieval woodland anywhere near London. A feature of east London which is of particular interest to children is the city farms, which are quite rare elsewhere.

As regeneration of the 'East End proper' takes hold, however, some very notable attractions are springing up. Canary Wharf, the largest office development in Europe, has given the Isle of Dogs Britain's tallest building, at 50 storeys high. The redevelopment of **St Katharine's Dock** has created what is by far the nicest marina in inner London – on a sunny day, it's a really charming place. The continuing efforts to improve the **Lee Valley** are beginning to make it an amenity which offers a large range of attractions.

The area is well served with non-commercial art galleries (the **Whitechapel Gallery** being the grandest and longest established).

For people-watching and browsing, the area has several of London's most characterful markets – **Petticoat Lane** and **Brick Lane**, and **Columbia Road Flower Market**, which are particularly popular Sunday morning destinations, and can be joined together on an interesting stroll (especially if you take in the former Truman Brewery on Brick Lane, which has been funkily redeveloped into a series of retail and gallery spaces with cafés and bars).

A trip on the (overground) Docklands Light Railway (from Bank or Tower Hill; www.dlr.co.uk) is an ideal way to see the much of the area. Travel is free if you have a Travelcard and, at weekends, a running commentary points out all the old dock areas and London's original Chinatown at Limehouse. End your trip in Greenwich and explore (see South London).

Essex Tourist Information Centre, Essex
County Hall, Market Rd, Chelmsford   (01245) 283400
 / *Times: Mon-Sat 10am-5pm (Sat 4pm); www.essexcc.gov.uk; BR: Chelmsford.*

Redbridge Tourist Information Centre, Essex
Clements Rd, Ilford   (020) 8708 2420
 / *Times: Mon-Fri 9.30am-8pm (Sat 4pm); www.redbridge.gov.uk; BR: Ilford.*

Indoor attractions

Association of Photographers Gallery EC2
81 Leonard St   (020) 7739 3631   5–1C
*A contemporary photographic gallery, holding 10-12 temporary
exhibitions annually. / Times: Mon-Fri 10.0 0am- 5.00pm, Sat 12pm-4pm;
www.aophoto.co.uk; Tube: Old Street.*

Bethnal Green Museum of Childhood E2
Cambridge Heath Rd   (020) 8983 5200   1–2D
*Housing the V&A's collection of toys, games, puppets, dolls and
dolls houses (of which there are over 40), this repository of
children's memorabilia offers quite enough to interest children
and parents. There are free workshops for children on most
Saturdays and Sundays, and school holiday activities. The
museum has an excellent supply of free literature about
London attractions, particularly those in the East End.
/ Times: Mon-Thu, Sat-Sun 10am-5.50pm; Tube: Bethnal Green; Café.*

Brooking Collection, Kent
University of Greenwich (Avery Hill), Bexley Rd, Eltham
(020) 8331 9100
*Windows rescued from Windsor, doorknobs from 10 Downing
Street …, this unique and comprehensive collection, amassed
by Charles Brooking over 35 years, contains over 100,000
architectural details from the past five centuries includes doors,
staircase sections, bootscrapers and rainwater heads. Many
visitors to the collection come because they inhabit a period
property which they want to restore or refurbish and want a
point of reference. Information on more than 7,000 items is
held on computer and examples of details of specific types or
particular periods can be retrieved prior to the visit. / Times: by
appointment, 9am-5pm (also weekends & evenings for groups); BR: .*

Chisenhale Gallery E3
64 Chisenhale Rd   (020) 8981 4518   1–2D
*This contemporary gallery holds half a dozen mixed media
shows a year by British and foreign artists. Many of the British
artists shown here have subsequently been nominated for the
prestigious Turner Prize. / Times: Wed-Sun 1pm-6pm;
www.chisenhale.org.uk; Tube: Mile End, Bethnal Green.*

Clowns Gallery E8
The All Saints Centre, Haggerston Rd   (020) 7608 0312
1–1D
*As the name suggests, you will find all sorts of artefacts and
archive material relating to clowns at this museum/gallery
opposite the All Saints Church. The evening of the first Tue in
the month is a 'social' with speakers and films, for example, on
subjects of clownish interest – donations greatly appreciated.
/ Times: 1st Tue of month 6.30pm-10.30pm, 1st Fri of month 12pm-5pm;
other times by arrangement including groups of up to 50 (Note: For large
groups, there will be a small charge.); www.clowns-international.co.uk;
BR: Highbury & Islington, London Fields BR.*

Geffrye Museum E2

Kingsland Rd   (020) 7739 9893   1–2D

This is a rather special museum, situated in elegant early c18 almshouses, which tells the story of English domestic interiors through a series of period rooms from Elizabethan times to the 1990s. There's also an enchanting walled herb garden and a fine display of period gardens, showing a visual history of town gardens over the past four hundred years. In summer the museum organises unusual, intelligent activities for kids and there is often music (not always period), inside or in the garden – ask for a programme. Most Londoners will never have been here – they should go. / Times: Tue-Sat 10am-5pm, Sun & bank hols 12pm-5pm; www.geffrye-museum.org.uk; Tube: Liverpool Street, Old Street; Restaurant.

Hackney Museum E8

Mare St   (020) 8986 6914   1–1D

The museum was established in 1986 to collect and preserve evidence regarding the history of Hackney from Viking times. It moved to new premises in Spring 2002 and now boasts state of the art displays, an education room and artefact stores. It's the displays that reflect the area's cultural diversity which are the particular attraction. Perhaps of special interest to local residents is 'Hackney Voices', a CD-ROM of information, photographs and interviews with first-generation Hackney residents about their experiences of settling in the borough. / Times: Mon-Sat 10am-5pm; www.hackney.gov.uk/hackneymuseum; BR: Hackney Central.

Hazle Ceramics Workshop*

Stallion's Yard, Codham Hall, Great Warley, nr Brentwood (01277) 220892

See how an award-winning range of collectable ceramic wall plaques is made. (If you decide you want to participate, there's a small charge.) / Times: Fri-Sat & bank hol Mon 11am-5pm; www.hazle.com; BR: Brentwoood (then 265 bus).

London Ambulance Service Museum, Essex

North East Sector HQ, Aldborough Rd South, Ilford (020) 8557 1767

It includes more than 20 vehicles – ranging from the horse-drawn ambulance of 1870 to a paramedic motorcycle of 1991 – but the museum also places much emphasis on the human aspects of the ambulance service. Curiosities include a first aid box that belonged to Prince Albert. / Times: by appt Mon-Fri 9.30am-4pm; www.londonambulance.nhs.uk/; Tube: Newbury Park.

London Chest Hospital E2

3rd Floor, Bonner Rd, Victoria Park   (020) 8983 2212   1–2D

The Capel Collection consists of 25 instruments and books of/on instruments relating to chest medicine collected since the Hospital was founded in 1848. There is a larger, more general collection at Royal London Hospital (see also). / Times: by appointment; Tube: Bethnal Green or D3 bus.

Matt's Gallery E3
42-44 Copperfield Rd   (020) 8983 1771   1–2D
This contemporary gallery commissions works ranging from installations which are made in – and specifically for – the space, to video, photography and painting exhibitions. Call for details of exhibitions. / Times: Wed-Sun 12pm-6pm (exhibitions); www.mattsgallery.org; Tube: Mile End.

North Woolwich Old Station Museum & Miniature Railway E16
Pier Rd   (020) 7474 7244
The museum is a Grade II listed Victorian station and platform, with locomotives, carriages, models and memorabilia. It tells the story of how the building of the Great Eastern Railway brought many changes to the area. There are quizes and interactive displays for children, and a miniature railway which runs on the first and second weekends of the month. School visits can be pre-booked for weekdays. / Times: Sat & Sun 1pm-5pm and every afternoon during Newham School holidays, closed in Dec; www.newham.gov.uk; BR: North Woolwich.

Plashet Zoo E7
Plashet Park, Shrewsbury Rd   (020) 8503 5994
If you would like to see animals more exotic than you would normally find in a city farm, why not visit the collection here – all year round, you can laugh at the llamas, wave at the wallabies, ogle the owls and gawp at the goats. In summer you can see tropical butterflies emerging (May-Sep) as well as falconry displays. Other reasons to visit include the Pheasant Garden and aviary. Donations are encouraged. / Times: summer Tue-Sun 10am-5pm; winter Tue-Sun 10am-4pm; Tube: East Ham; Café.

Ragged School Museum E3
46-50 Copperfield Rd   (020) 8980 6405   1–2D
This museum of the history of the East End is housed in a Victorian canalside warehouse which, from 1895, formed part of the largest ragged (free) school in London. Appropriately, education and the life and work of Dr Barnardo are given particular emphasis, and there is a recreated Victorian classroom (which is used by school groups for re-enacted Victorian lessons). On the first Sun of the month there are family arts and crafts workshops. During the school holidays, activities are organised, from making Victorian sweets to treasure hunts. All are popular and space is limited – call for a free programme. / Times: Wed & Thu 9am-5pm, 1st Sun of month 2pm-5pm; www.raggedschoolmuseum.org.uk; Tube: Mile End; Café.

Royal London Hospital Archives & Museum* E1
St Augustine with St Philip's Church, Newark St
(020) 7377 7608   1–2D
*The permanent exhibition about the history of the famous
hospital is housed in the basement of a c19 church. Highlights
include a small Hogarth drawing, George Washington's false
teeth, nursing uniforms from the 1900s, documents relating to
Elephant Man Joseph Merrick (and a copy of his hat) and a
bust of WWI heroine Edith Cavell (who trained here), as well
as her last letters from her condemned cell and the flag that
covered her coffin. There are also videos, including films from
the 1930s showing what it was like being a nurse and a
patient then.* / Times: Mon-Fri 10am-4.30pm (occasionally closed
1pm-2pm); www.brclf.org.uk; Tube: Whitechapel; Café, Restaurant, Picnic area.

The Showroom E2
44 Bonner Rd   (020) 8983 4115   1–2D
*As at the other two galleries nearby (Matt's and the
Chisenhale), the contemporary works displayed here are often
installation-based, but may include performance art and videos.
There are four exhibitions per year, lasting five weeks each. Call
for exhibition information.* / Times: Wed-Sun 1pm-6pm (exhibitions);
www.theshowroom.org; Tube: Bethnal Green.

Spitalfields Market E1
Brushfield St   (020) 7247 8556   5–2D
*The City's former fruit and vegetable market (vacated in 1991)
has been transformed into a mixed development that is a
particularly popular Sunday destination. At the heart of the
market are stalls selling arts and crafts, bric-à-brac, the latest
fashions and organic food. Spitalfields makes a great lunch stop
as there is an International Food Village, (with offerings from
Mexican chilli to Turkish kebabs). Regular special events include
an alternative fashion week, a dog show, a community festival
and a harvest festival. (Note: in a few years, this may revert to
being a food market – one plan being considered by the
Corporation of London is to consolidate Smithfield's Meat
Market, Billingsgate Fish Market and a fruit and veg market
here.)* / Times: Mon-Fri 10am-6pm, Sun 10am-5.30pm; Tube: Liverpool
Street.

Thames Police Museum E1
Marine Support Unit, 98 Wapping High St
(020) 7275 4421   1–3D
*This collection documents the history of the Marine Police;
artefacts date from 1798 – the date of the first organised
London police force. Weapons, including cutlasses, model boats
and uniforms, are all displayed in a pleasant setting overlooking
the Thames.* / Times: by written appointment, groups & clubs preferred;
Tube: Wapping.

Thurrock Museum, Essex
Thameside Complex, Orsett Rd, Grays   (01375) 652403
*A permanent gallery of the history of the Thurrock area,
displaying archaeology from the Stone Age to the medieval
period. There are also regularly changing temporary exhibitions
based on local themes. / Times: Mon-Sat 9am-5pm;
www.thurrock.gov.uk/museum; BR: Grays.*

Upminster Tithe Barn, Agricultural & Folk Museum, Essex
Hall Ln, Upminster   (01708) 447535
*The barn is a large thatched, timber-framed structure, probably
built around 1420. It contains a collection illustrating the
farming, urban and social history of the community and shows
the transition of the area from countryside to suburbia. There
are over 13,000 exhibits, including old agricultural implements,
farriers' tools, dairying equipment, bicycles, photographs,
laundry paraphernalia (from the time when it was all done
manually) and toys and games. / Times: 1st full weekend of each
month Apr-Oct, 2pm-6pm; www.upminster.com; BR: Upminster (then 248 bus);
(light refreshment stand).*

Upminster Windmill, Essex
St Mary's Ln, Upminster   (01708) 772394
*This white five-storey mill was built in the early c19 and worked
commercially until around 1935. It is owned by the London
Borough of Havering and staffed by members of Hornchurch &
District Historical Society. The mill has undergone substantial
repair, and it is hoped to have it working again in due course.
/ Times: Apr-Sep, 3rd Sat & Sun of month, 2pm-5.30pm;
www.upminster.com/upminster/history/windmill.htm; BR: Upminster Station;
Tube: Upminster.*

Valence House Museum, Essex
Becontree Av, Dagenham   (020) 8270 6865
*This partly-moated, c17 manor house, contains various locally
discovered artefacts dating from the Stone Age onwards. Its
most notable contents, perhaps, are fine portraits of the
Fanshawe family, including some by Lely and Kneller. There are
also domestic interiors from the c17 and c20, displays on the
history of Dagenham Village, and a walled herb garden.
Children's workshops are held periodically. / Times: Mon-Fri
9am-4.40pm Sat 10am- 4pm; www.lbbd.gov.uk/4-valence/valence-menu.html;
BR: Chadwell Heath; Tube: Becontree; Café (open Sat only).*

Vestry House Museum E17
Vestry Rd, Walthamstow   (020) 8509 1917
*This prettily-situated workhouse (1730) was converted into a
museum of local history in the 1930s. It is in the old village of
Walthamstow (which is worth a visit in its own right). The most
singular exhibit is probably the Bremer Car, which is claimed to
be one of the first petrol-driven cars to be made in London. An
original police cell (used between 1840 and 1870) is another
curiosity. There is a programme of temporary exhibitions.
/ Times: Mon-Fri 10am-1pm, 2pm-5.30pm (Sat 5pm), closed bank hols;
www.lbwf.gov.uk/leisure/intro/vestry_intro.stm; Tube: Walthamstow Central.*

Waltham Abbey Church, Essex

Highbridge St, Waltham Abbey   (01992) 767897

King Harold is said to be buried in the grounds of this Norman church, which was built in 1120 on the site of three previous churches. It was re-founded as an Augustinian abbey in 1177 by Henry II as part of his penance for the murder of Thomas Becket. The abbey was dissolved and partly destroyed in 1540 (the last in England to be closed by Henry VIII), leaving only the nave. The crypt centre contains shows an exhibition about the history of the town and abbey, which is close to Lee Valley Park (see also). / Times: 10am (12pm on Sun & 11am on Wed)-6pm (4pm in winter); www.walthamabbeychurch.co.uk; BR: Waltham Cross Station.

Whitechapel Art Gallery E1

80 Whitechapel High St   (020) 7522 7888,
recorded information (020) 7522 7878   5–2D

This important non-commercial venue, in its atmospheric Art Nouveau building, has no permanent collection. It can therefore make a virtue of necessity, presenting an ever-changing series of exhibitions of c20 and contemporary art, often of important and challenging artists. For details ring the recorded information line. There is generally a programme of talks around the exhibitions, and sometimes also early-evening films. / Times: Tue-Sun 11am-6pm (Thu 9pm); www.whitechapel.org; Tube: Aldgate East; Café.

William Morris Gallery E17

Lloyd Park, Forest Rd   (020) 8527 3782

William Morris, born in Walthamstow in 1834, was probably the most influential designer and craftsman London has ever produced. He died in 1896, but his ideas were carried on by the Arts and Crafts movement into the 1920s, and many of his designs, especially for wallpaper and fabric, are still in production today. This delightful c18 house in its own grounds contains a display of Morris's work and personal memorabilia, together with examples of the products of his associates, Burne-Jones, Rossetti and Philip Webb. / Times: Tue-Sat & 1st Sun of month 10am-1pm & 2pm-5pm; www.lbwf.gov.uk/wmg; Tube: Walthamstow Central; Picnic area.

Outdoor attractions

BBC Essex Garden, Essex

Crowther Nurseries, Ongar Rd, Abridge   (01708) 688581

The garden in which Ken Crowther tries out new products and techniques for the benefit of fans of his Saturday BBC radio show, Down to Earth, a garden magazine programme. Consisting of a vegetable plot, two small greenhouses, herbaceous and shrub borders, this garden is open to visitors even during filming for the show. If you time your visit accordingly, you may ask a question to which the answer may subsequently be broadcast. / Times: 9am-5.30pm; www.gardeningwithken.com; BR: Theydon Bois (then 500 bus); Café.

Brick Lane Market E1
1–2D
*Forget the papers – roll up early in the morning to start off
Sunday with a truly East End 'pile it high, sell it cheap'
experience. 'It' might be almost anything.* / Times: Sun 6am–1pm;
Tube: Aldgate, Aldgate East, Liverpool Street, Shoreditch; Café.

Canary Wharf E14
(020) 7418 2783 (box office/events information)   1–3D
*Cesar Pelli's great tower (244m high) on the Isle of Dogs is, at
50 storeys, the tallest building in Britain. You don't need to
approach it to appreciate it – you can see it from all over
London – but if you do, there's an impressive shopping mall at
its base with an ever-increasing number of shops and
restaurants. There are many other shiny, new buildings around
the tower's base, which are worth a view – over 5 million
square feet of office and retail space has been created and
occupied in the area since 1991. The public spaces are well-
kept and provide many different views of the tower: look for
the fountain in Cabot Square, which is controlled by a
computer that changes the water level if it's windy to stop
people getting sprayed. There is a regular programme of arts
and events, many of which are free, including outside events in
the summer. The towers that now flank Pelli's behemoth were
completed in 2001.* / www.canarywharf.com; Tube: Canary Wharf (DLR);
Café, Restaurant

Columbia Road Flower Market E2
Columbia Rd   5–1D
*Every Sunday morning this east London street (with a few
neighbouring alleys) bursts into bloom – you'll know you are
near the market when you see the occasional palm tree
walking down the street, possibly in the company of shrubs and
boxes of herbs. It's best to arrive early – it all gets terribly
crowded. A trip here combines well with a visit to Spitalfields
Market and Brick Lane.* / Times: Sun 8am–2pm; Tube: Old Street,
Liverpool Street, Shoreditch.

East Ham Nature Reserve E6
Norman Rd   (020) 8470 4525
*The two suburban nature trails here have the mission of
introducing everyone to the joys of nature. Set in London's
largest churchyard (in use since Norman times, though the
oldest stones date from the c17), the trails are fully accessible
(including to people in wheelchairs). A highly informative,
illustrated guide is available from the Visitor Centre – a Braille
version is also available. Ring to ensure the reserve is open
before you set off.* / Times: Tue-Fri 10am-5pm, Sat & Sun 2pm-5pm
(winter 1pm-4pm); Tube: East Ham.

Epping Forest, Essex
(020) 8508 0028

Two miles by 12, this ancient forest on the eastern fringe of London (owned by the Corporation of London since Victorian times) is the largest public open space in Essex. Great effort is put into maintaining the landscape, with its diverse natural history, and the area is designated as a Site of Special Scientific Interest. Although the forest is a very popular destination, it's big enough that you can lose yourself in it – real countryside AND accessible from a tube station! A particular attraction is Queen Elizabeth's Hunting Lodge (small charge to visit), near Chingford, which is the only surviving Tudor 'hunt-standing' (from which the monarch could view the hunt's progress). The information centre at High Beech organises occasional walks through the forest (details from the number given). At this spot (it's around two miles from Loughton), there is an easy-access path and also tracks that are popular with horse riders and mountain bikers. / Times: information centre, summer, 10am (Sun 11am)-5pm; winter, Mon-Fri 11am-3pm, Sat &Sun 10am (Sun 11am)-dusk; www.cityoflondon.gov.uk; Tube: Epping, Theydon Bois, Loughton, Snaresbrook, Debden.

Flitch Way
Rayne Station Centre, Station Rd, Rayne (01376) 340262

The Flitch Way is a country park passing through 15 miles of countryside along the former Bishop's Stortford to Braintree railway line. Your journey passes wildlife-rich railway cuttings, Victorian stations, farmland, villages and woodland. The Centre has an exhibition room of local history, open on Sundays. / Times: centre-Mon-Sat 8am-5pm, Sun 1pm-4pm; www.essexcc.gov.uk; BR: Braintree; Picnic area.

The Greenway
(020) 8472 1430 (ask for Park & Leisure Services)

Formerly less romantically described as the Northern Outfall Sewer Embankment, this elevated feature of the landscape was built in the 1860s to provide a sewage and drainage system for east London. Shedding its original image, the four mile long path now has been developed as a wildlife habitat and provides unfettered open spaces for walkers and cyclists. The route begins from Royal Dock Road in E6, and runs to Stratford High Road in E15 and beyond into Hackney. Along the entire route, there are access points for visitors and noticeboards about native flora and fauna. / Times: 6am-dusk; www.newham.gov.uk; Tube: Beckton (DLR), West Ham; Café, Restaurant, Picnic area.

Greenwich Foot Tunnel E14
(020) 8854 8888 ext 5493 (to confirm lift times)   1–3D
*The tunnel, opened in 1902, connects Greenwich with the Isle
of Dogs and was built because the steamboat ferry was
contributing to excessive congestion of the river at this point. It
lies 10 metres below the low water mark, is 390m long and is
made of cast iron segments, lined with concrete and tiled. New
lifts were installed in 1992, replacing equipment which had
lasted since 1904. After 1999, when the Jubilee Line opened
between Greenwich and Canary Wharf, the practical function
of the tunnel was somewhat overshadowed, although the
appeal of walking under the Thames continues to attract
children of all ages. / Times: lift service, Mon-Sat 7am-7pm, Sun
10am-5.30pm; tunnel 24 hours; www.greenwich.gov.uk; Tube: Greenwich,
Island Gardens (DLR).*

Hackney City Farm E2
1a Goldsmith's Row   (020) 7729 6381   1–2D
*Hackney City Farm keeps as full a range as possible of
traditional farm livestock in its one and a half-acre site. In
spring, the lambs and calves are a particular reason to take the
children. (On Wed, Thu and Sun, pottery-making is offered at a
rate of £2 an hour.) / Times: Tue-Sun 10am-4.30pm (& bank hols);
www.hackneycityfarm.co.uk; Tube: Bethnal Green; BR: Hackney; Café.*

Hainault Forest Country Park, Essex
(020) 8500 7353
*This square mile of woodland was dedicated to the public in
1906 and is one of the few remaining vestiges of the great
forest of Essex and Waltham (see also Epping Forest). It is a
Site of Special Scientific Interest because of the ancient
woodland, pollarded trees and flora and fauna. Foxburrows
Farm conserves rare breeds and employs traditional farm
practices. Activities in the summer events programme might
include a storytelling picnic, a fungi-finding expedition,
orienteering and a bat search. In the winter, there are bird-
feeding days and Christmas decorations workshops. There is a
brochure of events which can be obtained by calling the above
number. / Times: 7am-dusk; Tube: Hainault then 247 or 362 bus (or BR to
Romford or Ilford then 150 or 247 bus); Café.*

Hainault Lodge Nature Reserve, Essex
(020) 8500 7353 (Hainault Country Park)
*Redbridge Borough's first Local Nature Reserve is remarkable
for its views across London and for the variety of habitats
within its small area. You need to obtain permission and
arrange an appointment (from Pam and Tony Simpson, tel 020
8599 7818) to enter the 14-acre site (adjacent to the park),
but everyone is welcome and tours can be arranged. Creatures
you might see include many nesting birds and small mammals
– if you are very lucky you might spot the rare Black Rabbit.
/ Tube: Hainault then 247 or 362 bus (or BR to Romford or Ilford then 150 or
247 bus).*

Hatfield Forest, Herts

Estate Office, Takeley, Bishop's Stortford   (01279) 870678

This rare surviving example of a medieval royal hunting forest is a Site of Special Scientific Interest and a national nature reserve. The forest comprises over 400 hectares of ancient coppice woodland with two ornamental lakes, the c18 Shell House, a stream and a marsh reserve. / Times: Easter-Oct 31 10am-5pm; www.nationaltrust.org.uk; BR: Bishop's Stortford; Café, Picnic area.

Island History Trust E14

Docklands Settlement, 197 East Ferry Rd
(020) 7987 6041   1–3D

The Trust documents the social history of the Isle of Dogs, which has seen massive industrial growth, severe bomb damage, recession and, most recently, large-scale urban renewal. Five thousand pictures – from the 1870s to the 1960s – show street scenes, churches, sport, work, social lives, pubs and families. All are captioned and indexed and so of particular interest to people who have a connection with the area, or who wish to research family history. The area is named after a small island in the Thames which has long since disappeared – the site itself was never an island. / Times: Tue, Wed, and 1st Sun of every month 1.30pm-4.30pm; www.islandhistory.org.uk; Tube: Island Gardens (DLR), Mudchute (DLR); Café, Restaurant, Picnic area.

Lee Valley Regional Park, Essex

Lee Valley Park Information Centre, Abbey Gardens,
Waltham Abbey, Essex EN9 1XQ   (01992) 702200

Since 1967, the derelict valley of the River Lee has been being transformed into over 1,000 acres of 'green chain', extending out from Hackney, via Tottenham and Enfield, to the more truly rural delights of Hertfordshire and Essex. You can walk the whole 23 miles on the towpath, or cycle it – it is part of the National Cycle Network linking Hertfordshire with Harwich. Natural attractions include a variety of bird life and a dragonfly sanctuary. Man-made items of interest include some pretty and historic c18 buildings, among them the largest restored tidal mill left standing in Britain (open Sun, 2pm-4pm, small charge, (020) 8215 0050) and the Clock Mill. Within the park, you can also find Lee Valley Walk, a 50-mile regional walking trail from London to Luton, and River Lee Country Park, where you might be lucky enough to spot the rare bittern or smew (bird hides are open to all on weekends). If you're planning a visit, contact the Countryside Centre to pick up relevant leaflets. All parts of the Park are easily accessible from the rail line which runs alongside. / Times: centre, April-Oct, 9.30am-5pm; Nov-Feb, Tue-Sun 10am-4.30pm; www.leevalleypark.com; Tube: Tottenham Hale; Picnic area.

Mudchute Park & Farm E14
Pier St   (020) 7515 5901   1–3D
The largest urban farm in London, this 32-acre site is the most significant open space on the Isle of Dogs. It includes a riding arena, fields, a wild section, a picnic area and woodlands. Because it's several times bigger than most of the other farms – complete with its own grassland for grazing – it can be run largely as if it were a small farm in the country. On the livestock front, the speciality here is sheep, of which a wide variety are kept, but there are also cattle, goats and pigs. Each year there is a family day in July. / Times: summer 9am-5pm; winter 10am-4.30pm; www.towerbridge.freeserve.co.uk/mud1.htm; Tube: Crossharbour (DLR), Mudchute (DLR); Café.

New Billingsgate Fish Market E14
Trafalgar Way, Isle of Dogs   (020) 7987 1118   1–3D
Though the name is an historic one, these days you have to journey to a decidedly modern structure on the Isle of Dogs to mingle with the merchants and buyers at the UK's largest inland fish market (with some 100 stalls). It sells on average 25,000 tonnes of fish and fish products every year. (The original building on Lower Thames Street – built in 1873 on a site that had been a market for centuries – still stands, but is used for offices nowadays. New Billingsgate may in the future move to a more central site, perhaps as part of the redevelopment of Spitalfields). / Times: Tues-Sat 5am-8.30am, Sun (shellfish only) 6am-8am; www.billingsgate-market.org.uk; DLR: .

Newham City Farm E16
King George Av   (020) 7476 1170
This four and a half-acre farm has a wide range of livestock, including a shire horse, a donkey, cows, pigs, sheep, goats, chickens, ducks and geese. It is well geared up for casual visitors – 50,000 people pass through the gates each year. Following expansion into the neighbouring King George V Park, there is now a visitor centre. / Times: Tue-Sun 10am-5pm (4pm winter) & bank hols (closed 1pm-2pm); Tube: Royal Albert (DLR), or Plaistow (then 262 bus); Picnic area.

Petticoat Lane E1
Certainly the best-known market in the East End, and possibly in London. The Sunday morning activity here is a phenomenon worth seeing whether or not you have any desire to invest in some of the low-cost clothes which are the market's speciality. / Times: Sun 9am-2pm; Tube: Liverpool Street, Aldgate.

Postman's Park EC1
Little Britain, King Edward St   5–2B
A tiny entrance opposite the National Postal Museum leads into a small and unprepossessing park with benches and grass. However, follow the path and you see a long wooden porch protecting what looks like the rear wall of a block of flats and a slightly raised patio. Set into the wall are around 50 memorials to 'heroic men and women', many with a story to tell, and on the south side of the park is Michel Ayrton's bronze Minotaur, added in 1973. / Tube: St Paul's, Barbican.

Riverside Walk
See the introduction of the South section for suggestions of interesting walks by the Thames.

St Katharine's Dock E1
1–3D
St Katharine's by the Tower (as the area is more properly called) is a fine collection of buildings, principally designed by the great c19 engineer Thomas Telford, restored to make a very attractive marina. It offers by far the nicest place for a riverside stroll in central London – the Tower of London and Tower Bridge provide a dramatic backdrop. In the summer, there is lunchtime music several times a week. / www.stkaths.co.uk; Tube: Tower Hill; Café.

Spitalfields Community Farm E1
Pedley St   (020) 7247 8762   1–2D
Despite its small size (one and a half-acres) and location (on former wasteground), this popular attraction manages to squeeze in most of the usual farm animals. Look out also for special events at Christmas and Easter, and during the summer, some of which are free. In addition, community members can take the National Proficiency Test Council Course (NPTC) in horticulture training for free. It begins in the spring and runs through autumn, averaging about 90 hours of training. / Times: Tue-Sun 10.30am-5pm; www.spitalfieldscityfarm.org; Tube: Aldgate East, Shoreditch.

Stepping Stones Farm E1
Stepney Way   (020) 7790 8204   1–2D
This eight-acre farm has all the main types of farm animals – cows, pigs, donkeys, sheep, goats, chickens, ducks and geese, as well as rabbits, guinea pigs and ferrets. There is also a picnic garden and play area. The venture, now in existence for over 20 years, is run entirely by volunteers and trainees, and partly funded by the sale of produce and home produce. Look out for events during school holidays (such as the Easter egg hunt), some of which are free. / Times: Tue-Sun 9am-6pm (dusk in winter); www.aboutbritain.com/steppingstonesfarm.htm; Tube: Stepney Green, Limehouse (DLR); Café.

Thorndon Country Park & Hartswood, Essex
(01277) 211250 (Essex Ranger Service)
A medley of parks, lakes, woods and golf clubs makes up this rural retreat, and there's lots of history and nature to wander through, including a deer park little changed since the c16. / Times: park: 8am-dusk; Countryside Centre: summer 10am-5pm, winter Tues-Sun & bank hol 10am-3.30pm; BR: Brentwood (then 151 bus to Halfway House or 73 bus to Warley).

Tower Hamlets Cemetery Park E3
Southern Gr   (020) 8983 5367   1–2D
*Built as a model necropolis for wealthy Londoners in 1841, this
27-acre site was used for burials up until 1966. A period of
neglect followed, during which the local flora and fauna
established themselves with a vengeance – in 1986, Tower
Hamlets decided to make a virtue of necessity and declared
the place a nature reserve, now boasting 20 species of
butterfly and some 35 types of bird. Some very fine Victorian
tombs remain, and there is also a tree trail, which takes about
45 minutes to complete.* / Times: 8.30am-dusk;
www.towerhamletscemetery.org; Tube: Mile End.

Victoria Park E3
Old Ford Rd   (020) 8985 1957   1–2D
*In the 1840s, concern grew in east London about the lack of
any recreational space for the burgeoning population. Fearing
unrest, the government sold York House in Westminster to pay
for the establishment of the new Victoria Park (of 220 acres) to
be a 'Green Lung' for the area. It is still the only large, formal
park in the East End. Its style is very much in keeping with its
name – it has lakes and fountains, one of which is a Gothic
drinking fountain from 1861, large areas of bedding plants, a
children's playground, a bandstand (with live music on Sunday
afternoons in July and August) and a herd of fallow deer.
Recent years have seen much refurbishment of the facilities.
The oldest model boat club in the world meets here most
Sunday mornings during the summer.* / Times: 7.30am-dusk;
Tube: Bethnal Green, Mile End.

Walthamstow Market E17
Walthamstow High St   1–1D
*Claiming to be the longest street market in Europe, this mile-
long stretch of stalls sells a plethora of wares from antiques to
designer clothes.* / Times: Mon-Fri 9am-4pm, Sat 9am-5pm;
Tube,BR: Walthamstow Central.

West Ham Park* E7
Upton Ln   (020) 8472 3584
*This 77-acre park in West Ham has been owned and run by
the Corporation of London since 1874. The recreational
facilities include a large children's playground, tennis courts and
a seven-acre formal garden in the south east corner of the
park. During the summer, there are children's entertainers at
the bandstand, and Sunday afternoon concerts.*
/ Times: 7.30am-30 mins before dusk; www.cityoflondon.gov.uk; Tube: Plaistow,
Stratford; Café, Restaurant, Picnic area.

Woolwich Free Ferry SE18
North Woolwich Pier, New Ferry Approach
(020) 8921 5786
*The ferry – the only free automated way to cross the Thames –
began in 1889. Paddlesteamers were, alas, replaced by the
current, less romantic, design in 1963.* / Times: 6.10am-8pm;
www.members.spree.com/SIP1/freeferry; BR: north of the Thames, North
Woolwich; south of the Thames Woolwich Arsenal, Woolwich Dockyard.

Maps

MAP I – LONDON OVERVIEW

Fryent Country Park

A

M1

A41

B

Golders Green Crematorium

NORTH

A5

Golders Hill Park

Map 4

Brent

Shri Swaminarayan Mandir

Hampstead

1

Grange Museum

Gladstone Park

Brent One Stop Shop

Stables Art Centre & Gallery

London International Gallery of Children's Art

West Hampstead

Wembley Market

North Circular Road A406

Wembley

Roundwood Park

Kilburn

Queen's Park

Regent Park

Brent Lodge Park

M

A40

Portobello Road Market

2

Acton

Bayswater Road Market

WEST

Notting Hill

Map 3

Pitshanger Manor Museum

Shepherds Bush Market

Holland Park

Gunnersbury Park Museum

Leighton House

Gunnersbury Triangle

Chiswick

3 M4

Narwhal Inuit Art Gallery

William Morris Society

Chelsea

Hogarth's House

Chiswick House

Public Record Office

Kew

Battersea

Fulham

Putney

4

Puppet Centre Trust

De Morgan Centre

Wandsworth Museum

Royal British Legion Poppy Factory

Wandsworth

Richmond Park

Richmond Park

Wimbledon Common

Wimbledon Society's Museum

MAP I – LONDON OVERVIEW

Waterlow Park

C   A10   D

Highgate

Lauderdale House Community Arts Centre

Railway Fields

Abney Park Cemetery

Stoke Newington

Walthamstow Market

Hackney Marshes

Clowns' Gallery
Hackney Museum

M102

Dalston

Camden

London Chest Hospital

Islington

Geffrye Museum   Victoria Park

Hackney City Farm   ark

Void Gallery

Chisenhale Gallery

The Showroom

Bethnal Green Museum of Childhood

EAST

Tower Hamlets Cemetery

2   Ragged School Museum

C   Map 5   Spitalfields Community Farm

Matt's Gallery

Stepney Stepping Stones Farm

E   City   Royal London Hospital Archives   ands

N   Brick Lane Market

St Katharine's Dock   A13

T   Thames Museum   Billingsgate

R   Canary Wharf

A   Pumphouse Museum

L   Southwark   Surrey Docks Farm

Island History Trust   Isle of Dogs

A3   Bermondsey Antiques Market

Cuming Museum   Mudchute Park & Farm

Beaconsfield Contemporary Art

Vauxhall City Farm   Greenwich Foot Tunnel

Livesey Museum   Cutty Sark

Greenwich Market

Chumleigh Gardens   Royal Naval College

New Covent Garden Market   erwell   Royal Arsenal   Greenwich

Greenwich Park

South London Art Gallery   Old Royal Observatory

A2

Blackheath

Age Exchange Reminiscence Centre

Brixton

Nunhead Cemetery

apham   Lewisham

SOUTH

Brixton Market

Photofusion   Dulwich

Black Cultural Museum

London Wildlife Garden Centre

Dulwich Park   Sydenham Hill Wood Local Nature Preserve

Dulwich Picture Gallery   Horniman Museum & Gardens

Belair Park

MAP 2 – CENTRAL LONDON

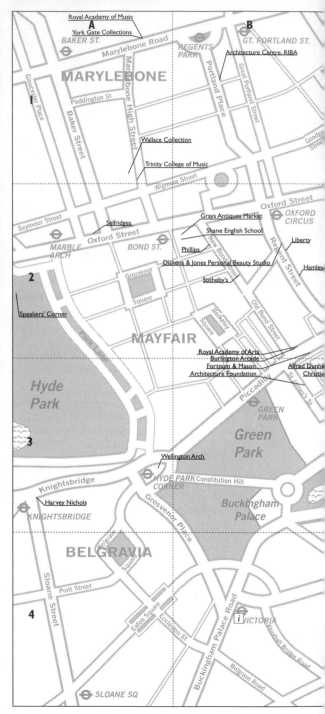

A B

Royal Academy of Music
York Gate Collections

BAKER ST.

Marylebone Road

REGENTS PARK

GT. PORTLAND ST.

Architecture Centre, RIBA

MARYLEBONE

Portland Place

Great Portland Street

Gloucester Place

Paddington St

Marylebone High Street

Baker Street

1

Goodge Street

Wallace Collection

Trinity College of Music

Wigmore Street

Oxford Street

OXFORD CIRCUS

Seymour Street

Grays Antiques Market

Shane English School

Selfridges

Oxford Street

Liberty

MARBLE ARCH

BOND ST.

Phillips

New Bond Street

Regent Street

Hamley

Dickens & Jones Personal Beauty Studio

Grosvenor

Sotheby's

2

Square

Speakers' Corner

Berkeley

Old Bond Street

Square

Park Lane

MAYFAIR

Royal Academy of Arts
Burlington Arcade
Fortnum & Mason
Architecture Foundation

Alfred Dunhi
Christie

Hyde Park

Piccadilly

St. James's St.

GREEN PARK

3

Green Park

Wellington Arch

Knightsbridge

HYDE PARK CORNER Constitution Hill

Harvey Nichols

Grosvenor Place

Buckingham Palace

KNIGHTSBRIDGE

BELGRAVIA

Belgrave Square

Sloane Street

Pont Street

4

Buckingham Palace Road

Eaton Square

Eccleston St.

i VICTORIA

Vauxhall Bridge Road

Belgrave Road

SLOANE SQ

MAP 2 – CENTRAL LONDON

C

D

Percival David Foundation of Chinese Art
RUSSELL SQ.
Guilford Street
Coram's Fields

University College Art Collection
Flaxman Gallery
Petrie Museum
Grant Museum
UCL Lunch Lectures

British Cartoon Centre
Gt Ormond St Hospital

BLOOMSBURY
Russell Square
Southampton Row

GOODGE

Gower Street
ottenham Court Road
Charlotte

Theobald's Road
Gray's Inn Road
Gray's Inn Road

BOC Museum
Architectural Association

Gray's Inn
CHANCERY LANE

British Museum

High Holborn

Contemporary Applied Art

Sir John Soane's Museum
HOLBORN

Lincoln's Inn

TOTTENHAM
COURT RD.

Chancery L

Berwick Street Market
Foyle's

Borders

London Silver Vaults

SOHO

Charing Cross Road

Freemason's Hall
COVENT
GARDEN

Royal Courts of Justice

Covent Garden Market
Royal Opera House
Theatre Museum

Shaftesbury Ave.

Twinings
Aldwych

COVENT
GARDEN

Somerset House

ALDWYCH
Roman Bath

LEICESTER SQ.

Photographer's Gallery
Courtauld Gallery
Gilbert Collection

Swiss Centre Clock
PICCADILLY
CIRCUS

National Portrait Gallery
St Martin in the Fields
London Brass Rubbing Centre
Cleopatra's Needle
Royal Society of Arts
Victoria Embankment Gardens

Strand
Waterloo Bridge

British Travel Centre

National Gallery

Haymarket

Regent St.

i

Canada House
Collectors Fair

Trafalgar
Square
EMBANKMENT

Royal Nat. Theatre

CHARING
CROSS

Northumberland Av.

Royal Festival Hall
South
Bank
Centre

ST JAMES'S

Pall Mall

Whitehall

Victoria Embankment

River Thames

WATERLOO

The Mall

St James's
Park

Horse Guards Parade

York Road

WESTMINSTER

rdcage Walk
ST. JAMES'S
PARK

Houses of Parliament

Westminster Bridge

LAMBETH
NORTH

Westminster Abbey

Houses
of
Parliament

Victoria Street

Blewcoat School
Westminster Cathedral

Westminster City Archives

Victoria Tower Gardens
Tibetan Peace Garden
Imperial War Museum

WESTMINSTER

Marsham St.

Lambeth Palace Road

Lambeth
Palace

London Scottish Regimental Museum
Horseferry Road

Museum of Garden History
Lambeth Br.

Lambeth Road

chester Row

PIMLICO

Tate Britain

Millbank

LAMBETH

MAP 3 – WEST LONDON (SW POSTCODES)

A **B**

Kensington Ch St

Kensington Gardens

KENSINGTON

Albert Memorial

Royal College of Art

i

I

Kensington High Street

Kensington Roof Gardens

Gloucester Road

Queensgate

Royal Albert Hall

HIGH ST. KENSINGTON

Royal College of Music

Holland Park

The Orangery and The Ice House

Baden-Powell House

Cromwell Road

GLOUCESTER RD

2

Earl's Court Road

EARLS COURT

Warwick Road

Old Brompton Road

Fulham Road

EARL'S COURT

Earl's Court Exhibition Centre

Lillie Road

Finborough Road

Redcliffe Gardens

3 WEST BROMPTON

Brompton Cemetery

North End Road Market

FULHAM BROADWAY

Fulham Road

4 FULHAM

Chelsea Harbour

New King's Road

MAP 3 – WEST LONDON (SW POSTCODES)

MAP 4 – NORTH LONGON

Kenwood House

A

B

HIGHGATE

Hampstead
Heath

Spaniards Rd

N. End Way

I

Highgate Ponds

Hampstead Ponds

Burgh House

HAMPSTEAD

HAMPSTEAD

Highgate Rd

Parliament Hills Lido

High St

Rosslyn Hill

Fleet Road

Mansfield Rd

Camden Arts Centre

Fitzjohn's Ave

BELSIZE
PARK

Haverstock Hill

KENTISH
TOWN

Malden Rd

Kentish Town City Farm

2

FINCHLEY RD.

CHALK FARM

Chalk Farm Rd

Camden Market

SWISS
COTTAGE

Adelaide Road

Camden Lock

CAMDEN TOWN

Finchley Road

Primrose Hill

Camden

Parkway

Albany Street

ST JOHN'S WOOD

Avenue Rd

Prince Albert Rd

ST. JOHN'S WOOD

3

Wellington Road

Abbey Rd

Ben Uri Museum

Regent's Park

St John's Wood Rd

Maida Vale

Park Road

Royal College of Physicians

Edgware Road

MARYLEBONE

BAKER ST.

GT. PORTLAND

REGENT'S
PARK

4

Marylebone Road

WESTWAY

EDGWARE
RD.

MARYLEBONE

Baker Street

Praed St

Edgware Road

Sussex Gdns

PADDINGTON

MAP 4 – NORTH LONDON

C
D

FINSBURY PARK

Finsbury Park

FINSBURY PARK

Hornsey Road

Seven Sisters Rd

Blackstock Rd

ARCHWAY

ARSENAL

TUFNELL PARK

Parkhurst Rd

HOLLOWAY RD.

Holloway Road

Brecknock Rd

KENTISH TOWN

Camden Road

CALEDONIAN RD.

Freightliners Farm

Islington Museum Gallery

Liverpool Road

HIGHBURY AND ISLINGTON

CAMDEN ROAD

Caledonian Road

Upper Street

York Way

St Pancras Way

BTCV

Camley Street Natural Park

ISLINGTON

Essex Road

CAMDEN TOWN

MORNINGTON CRESCENT

Pancras Rd

Chapel Market

Crafts Council

ANGEL

Eversholt Street

KING'S CROSS

Pentonville Road

City Road

Hampstead Rd

British Library

Euston Road

Oak Room

London Metropolitan Archives

EUSTON

i

Gray's Inn Rd

Farringdon Rd

Two10 Gallery

WARREN ST.

Wellcome Trust

EUSTON SQ.

BLOOMSBURY

RUSSELL SQ.

FARRINGDON

Tottenham Court Rd

Theobald's Rd

CHANCERY LANE

GOODGE ST.

High Holborn

HOLBORN

Oxford Street

TOTTENHAM COURT ROAD

OXFORD CIRCUS

Fleet St

MAP 5 – THE CITY

A

B

Mount Pleasant Royal Mail Sorting Office

Family Record Centre

John St

Old Street

St John's Gate, Amb' exhibition,
Order's Library & Museum

Clerkenwell Road

I

The Clerk's Well

Farringdon Rd

FARRINGDON

BARBICAN

Beech St

Barbican

Leather Lane Market

Charterhouse St

Smithfield Market

Aldersgate St

Gray's Inn

St Etheldreda

EC1

Holborn

Smithfield Market

Museum of London

London V

Mus. of St Bartholomew's Hosp'

City Yeomanry Museum

Old Bailey

Postman's Park

Gresham St

2

Lincoln's Inn

Newgate St

Museums of the Royal College of Surgeons

Prince Henry's Room

ST. PAUL'S

Cheapside

Fleet St

Farringdon Road

Ludgate Hill

City Information Office

i

Cannon Street

EC4

*MANSION
HOUSE*

Inner Temple

College of Arms

Middle Temple

Queen Victoria St

Salvation Army International Heritage Centre

BLACKFRIARS

Victoria Embankment

Upper Thames St

Blackfriars Br

3

River Thames

Southwark Br

OXO Tower

Tate Modern

Bargehouse

Stamford St

SOUTHWARK

Southwark St

Blackfriars Rd

Southwark Bridge Rd

4

WATERLOO

Union Street

Jerwood Space

Waterloo Road

The Cut

BOROUGH

MAP 5 – THE CITY

C

D

Wesley's Chapel

Columbia Road Flower Market

Association of Photographers Gallery

FINSBURY

HAC (Bunhill Fields)

Museum of the HAC

Bunhill Row

City Rd

Gt Eastern

Commercial St

Chiswell St

Guildhall School of Music & Drama

Bishopsgate

Broadgate

Spitalfields Market

MOORGATE

Finsbury Circus

LIVERPOOL ST.

Bishopsgate

Middlesex St

EC2

Chartered Insurance Institute

Clockmakers' Company Collection

Guildhall Library

Guildhall

Guildhall Art Gallery

Houndsditch

ALDGATE

Bank of England Museum

Threadneedle St

Whitechapel Art Gallery

Aldgate

BANK

Cornhill

Leadenhall St

Leadenhall Market

King William St

Gracechurch St

Fenchurch St

MONUMENT

FENCHURCH ST.

Cannon Street

CANNON ST.

The Monument

Eastcheap

Gt Tower St

TOWER HILL

Upper Thames St

EC3

Lower Thames St

Tower of London

Tower of London

London Br

River Thames

Winchester Palace

Southwark Cathedral

Borough Market

LONDON BRIDGE

City Hall

Tower Bridge

Borough High St

St Thomas St

Tooley Street

Bermondsey St

Tower Bridge Road

George Inn

BOROUGH

London Glass Blowing Workshop

Druid St

Long Lane

Index by type of attraction

Index by type of attraction

Index by type of attraction

Alphabetical index

Alphabetical index